D0152912

ALLEN & UNWIN, INC.

9 Winchester Terrace
Winchester, Massachusetts 01890
(617) 729-0830

takes pleasure in sending you this copy for review

Title: THE CYPRUS TRIANGLE

Author: Rauf Denktash

Price: Cloth-$17.95 (trade)

Publication date: August 15, 1982

Please refer to our U.S. address in your review
Two clippings will be greatly appreciated

The Cyprus Triangle

THE CYPRUS TRIANGLE

R. R. DENKTASH

Published jointly by
K. Rustem & Bro.
and
GEORGE ALLEN & UNWIN
London   Boston   Sydney

George Allen & Unwin (Publishers) Ltd,
40 Museum Street, London WC1A 1LU, UK

George Allen & Unwin (Publishers) Ltd,
Park Lane, Hemel Hempstead, Herts HP2 4TE, UK

Allen & Unwin Inc.,
9 Winchester Terrace, Winchester, Mass 01890, USA

George Allen & Unwin Australia Pty Ltd,
8 Napier Street, North Sydney, NSW 2060, Australia

K. Rustem & Bro.,
PO Box 239, Nicosia, Northern Cyprus

First published in 1982

British Library Cataloguing in Publication Data

Denktash, R. R.
    The Cyprus triangle.
    1. Cyprus – History   2. Cyprus – Politics and government
    I. Title
    956.45   DS54.95
    ISBN 0-04-327066-2

Library of Congress Cataloging in Publication Data

Denktash, R. R. (Rauf R.)
    The Cyprus triangle
Includes bibliographical references.
1. Cyprus – History. 2. Cyprus – Foreign relations –
Turkey. 3. Cyprus – Foreign relations – Greece.
4. Cyprus – Foreign relations – Great Britain. I. Title.
DS54.3.D44   956.45   82-6657
ISBN 0-04-327066-2   AACR2

Set in 11 on 13 point Baskerville by Bedford Typesetters Ltd,
and printed in Great Britain
by Billing and Sons Ltd, Guildford, London and Worcester

Contents

But at no time has the island been
a constituent part of Hellenic Greece.
It was absorbed, along with, but not as
an integral part of, Greece proper and
the Aegean area, by the Byzantine Empire.
Its church was an autocephalous member
of the Holy Eastern Orthodox Church, and
thus religion combined with language to
foster the idea that Cypriots were Greek
in origin.
(Sir George Hill, *History of Cyprus* (1952), Vol. 4, p. 488)

Introduction

There is not, and there has never been, a Cypriot nation. That may be the misfortune of Cyprus and indeed the root cause of its problem, but it is a reality which has to be faced and understood by all concerned.

When Cyprus acquired independence in August 1960 and later became a full member of the United Nations Organisation Archbishop Makarios, in his capacity as the Ethnarch of the Greek Cypriots, publicly declared that the Agreements had brought into being a state and not a nation. On 28 March 1963, the English-language newspaper, *Cyprus Mail*, carried this statement by Archbishop Makarios, who became the President of the bi-communal Republic of Cyprus: 'No Greek who knows me can ever believe that I would wish to work for the creation of a Cypriot national awareness. The Agreements have created a state but not a nation.' Unfortunately not only Greeks but also the Turkish Cypriots knew that Archbishop Makarios spoke in earnest.

Lacking nationhood and deprived of 'a Cypriot national awareness' the two national communities which had agreed to establish the bi-communal state in 1960 soon found themselves in political difficulties. On his election to the presidency of the Republic, Makarios told his bi-religious and bi-national subjects that 'for the first time in eight centuries the government of the island has passed into Greek hands'. Under the terms of the Agreements the government of the republic was to be shared between the two communities in Cyprus, and it had no time for such constitutional niceties.

The Greek Cypriot leaders chose to ignore the main objective of the 1960 Agreements which was to eliminate the Turkish Cypriots' fear of the union of Cyprus with Greece. Guarantees had been written into the Cypriot Constitution to safeguard the intercommunal partnership which had been established and to prevent the union of the island, in whole or in part, with any other country. For Archbishop Makarios the union of Cyprus with Greece (Enosis) was such an important and glorious objective that he believed that any means to this end were totally justified. International treaties and his position as the President of a bi-national republic, which was guaranteed against union with Greece, were not seen by Makarios as insurmountable obstacles. He made this clear when, as the first President of Cyprus, he made this public declaration on 5 January 1962:

> The noble struggles of the people never come to an end. These struggles, although they undergo transformation, are never terminated. The struggle of the people of Cyprus, too, will go on.
>
> The Zurich and London Agreements form a landmark in the course of this struggle, but, at the same time, are a starting-point and bastion for further struggles, with the object of capitalising on what has been achieved for further conquests.

During the course of a sermon at Kykko Monastery on 15 August 1962, he reiterated that Enosis was his aim:

> Greek Cypriots must continue to march forward to complete the work began by the EOKA heroes. The struggle is continuing in a new form, and will go on until we achieve our goal.

Years later, during the intercommunal conflict which was

the inevitable consequence of the Enosis idea, Makarios declared on 14 March 1971 at Yialousa:

Cyprus is Greek. Cyprus has been Greek since the dawn of its history, and it will remain Greek.
Greek and undivided we have taken it over,
Greek and undivided we shall preserve it.
Greek and undivided we shall deliver it to Greece.

In the same year, on 29 October 1971, the Greek Cypriot press reported this statement from the archbishop:

I can now disclose that I have stated clearly and categorically to Greek governments from time to time that I would unhesitatingly proclaim Enosis, if I had the consent to this end, that is if Greece were prepared to accept Enosis and share the responsibilities for the repercussions from such a venture.

To those who doubted his sincerity on Enosis, Archbishop Makarios told *Le Point* on 19 February 1973:

I have struggled for the union of Cyprus with Greece, and Enosis will always be my deep national aspiration as it is the aspiration of all Greek Cypriots. My national creed has never changed and my career as a national leader has showed no inconsistency or contradiction. I have accepted independence instead of Enosis because certain external conditions and factors have not allowed a free choice.

Makarios identified the Turkish Cypriots as the main obstacle to his Enosis aspirations. On 4 September 1963, just three months before he ordered his forces to attack them, he said: 'Unless this small Turkish community forming a part of the Turkish race which has been the terrible enemy of

Hellenism is expelled, the duty of the heroes of EOKA can never be considered as terminated.'

For the Turkish Cypriot partners of the bi-national state, the alternative to resistance to Enosis was submission to the will of the Greek Cypriots and the eventual acceptance of the colonisation of Cyprus by Greece. The 1955–8 struggle was caused by the Greek Cypriot attempt to achieve union with Greece and the Turkish Cypriot objection to this. The compromise settlement, on the basis of a bi-national state guaranteed against union of any kind and guaranteeing the partnership rights of the Turkish community, would either be cherished and honoured, or destroyed. The Greek Cypriot leaders chose to destroy this partnership state and sought to establish a purely Greek Cypriot administration by ejecting the Turkish Cypriot elements from the government. The 1963 Greek Cypriot onslaught on the Turkish Cypriot community was the inevitable result of the Greek Cypriots' pursuit of the dream of Enosis. The Turkish Cypriot resistance between 1963–74 and the Turkish intervention of 1974, however, effectively prevented the implementation of this absurd scheme.

In the following pages an attempt has been made, in as objective a manner as possible, to state facts giving, wherever possible, full references for the sources of information. I have tried to keep out of the picture as much as possible because this is not an autobiography but a factual assessment of the Cyprus problem.

Lastly, a word of appreciation and thanks to my friend Mr Zafer Zihni, without whose help and encouragement *The Cyprus Triangle* would not have been written, and to Mr Kemal Rüstem for his efforts to publish the book in association with Allen & Unwin.

RAUF R. DENKTASH

1 Introducing Cyprus

Cyprus is the third largest island in the Mediterranean with an area of 3,572 square miles, lying 40 miles south of Turkey, 77 miles west of Syria, 300 miles south of the United Arab Republic and 650 miles south-east of Greece. Two ranges of mountains, Troödos in the south and Pendadaktilos in the north, border the dry Messaoria plain which extends from Morphou Bay to Famagusta. The highest peak is 6,401 ft (Mount Olympus) on Troödos where, during the winter, skiing is a popular sport.

The population of Cyprus consists of 24·6 per cent Turkish Cypriots and 74·7 per cent Greek Cypriots (Turkish Cypriot census 1973). Small groups of Maronites, Latins, Armenians, British ex-patriates and others make up the rest of the population. Greek Cypriots belong to the Greek Orthodox Church and speak Greek; Turkish Cypriots are Sunni Moslems and speak Turkish.

Each community has its own system of education conducted in its own language and there is no intermarriage between the two communities who have maintained and jealously guarded their respective cultural and national heritages over four centuries of coexistence in the island.

2 *Early History*

The Turks conquered Cyprus from the Venetians in 1571 in order to end the piracy on the Eastern Mediterranean trade routes and to eliminate the danger to Ottoman interests posed by the foreign possession of this island which commanded a strategically important position in the area. The Turks terminated the Latin persecution of the Greek-speaking Christians in the island and reactivated the Greek Orthodox Church with all its rights and privileges. Turkish rule continued until 1878. In that year, through a bilateral treaty, the Ottoman Empire allowed Great Britain to take over the administration of the island while it continued to retain sovereignty over it, in return for a British promise to support Turkey in the event of a Russian attack on her.

The island was annexed by Great Britain in 1914, however Turkey did not recognise this until the Treaty of Lausanne in 1923. The first British governor, Sir Garnet Wolseley, had landed in Cyprus on 22 July 1878 and the last British Governor, Sir Hugh Foot (now Lord Caradon) finally left the island on 16 August 1960. On that day, Cyprus became a bi-national republic as a result of the agreements in February 1959 in Zurich and London between the interested parties, that is the Turkish Cypriots, Turkey, the Greek Cypriots, Greece and Great Britain.

3 *Agitation for Enosis*

On the day the first British governor landed in Cyprus, the then Bishop of Kitium, Kyprianos, formally asked for the union of Cyprus with Greece, that is to say Enosis.[1] The Turkish Cypriot leaders of the time contended that Cyprus was not Greek, had never been part of Greece and therefore could not be given to Greece. Thus the seeds of future inter-communal discord were sown on the fertile soil of Cyprus.

The Greek Cypriot Church had begun to agitate for union with Greece as early as 1825, but its preparations for an insurrection against Turkish rule had been quickly put down by the then Ottoman governor. The political agitation of the church continued after the advent of British rule. Towards the end of the nineteenth century Crete, another Turkish island in the Mediterranean, had been granted self-rule by the Ottoman Empire. Soon afterwards the Turkish population of Crete was either massacred or forced to flee and Crete united with Greece. 'The Cretan struggle' was to be a model for the 'Cyprus struggle' as envisaged by the Greek Orthodox Church.[2] Greece had sent school-teachers, lawyers, doctors and priests to Cyprus in order to foment nationalism amongst the Greek-speaking population. In 1931 there was an abortive uprising for union with Greece (Enosis). As a result, the British suspended all popular representation in the administration of the colony and imposed strict restrictions on all nationalistic activities. Thus Turkish Cypriots were deprived of their legitimate rights because of Greek fanaticism. Moreover, Turkish Cypriots were subjected to even more vigorous suppression than the Greek Cypriots.

This state of affairs continued until the end of the Second World War in 1945. The leaders of the 1931 insurrection returned to the island from exile in Greece after the war and resumed their militant activities for uniting the island with Greece. This immediately provoked a reaction from the Turkish Cypriots who strongly objected to such a union.

1950 was a significant year in the Greek Orthodox Church's campaign for Enosis. In that year the Church organised a plebiscite for Enosis. Open registers were placed in churches and all Greek Cypriots were invited to sign, either in favour of or against union with Greece, while the local priests looked on. In the same year, Archbishop Makarios III, then aged 37, was enthroned as the new Archbishop of Cyprus. He declared on enthronement that he would devote all his energies to achieving Enosis during his lifetime.[3] He kept his Enosis pledge known as 'the holy oath', and caused much strife and bloodshed, intercommunal as well as inter-Greek, in Cyprus until his death on 3 August 1977.

4 *British Offers of Self-Rule*

In 1948, under Lord Winster's governorship, the British government offered self-government to Cyprus. The Greek Orthodox Church rejected this offer on the grounds that self-government would be the grave of Enosis. Turkish Cypriots were willing to accept self-government provided that Enosis was effectively barred; the Turkish community's autonomous rights in education, religion and personal status, which had been abrogated by the British, were restored; and the Turkish community's participation in the administration was guaranteed as a precaution against further discrimination and oppression. The Communist Party (AKEL), which had agreed to participate in the negotiations for a constitution, had to withdraw as a result of pressure by the church, which was acting in full collusion with the government in Athens. Thus Archbishop Makarios's 'holy oath', to steer the Cyprus ship to the shores of Greece and achieve Enosis, was transformed from personal ambition to a national policy.

Later, the Greek Cypriot leadership rejected two more proposals for self-rule. In 1956, for example, they rejected the Radcliffe proposals for a constitution which envisaged 'a wide measure of responsible self-government'. The intransigence of the Greek Cypriots was due to the fact that they were planning to achieve Enosis quickly through a terror campaign against the British and the Turkish Cypriots and would not deviate from this plan.

5 EOKA Terror Campaign

In 1954, Greece brought the Cyprus problem before the United Nations, seeking the union of Cyprus with Greece through the one-sided application of the principle of 'self-determination'. Turkish Cypriots, supported by Turkey, vehemently objected to this move. The same year, Colonel George Grivas, a Greek national, landed in Cyprus with Greek arms and personnel in order to organise an underground movement for union with Greece. Grivas had been invited to Cyprus by Archbishop Makarios who had taken another, this time secret, oath in Athens in March 1953 to work for Enosis and face any danger as a member of this underground organisation.[4] All the resources of the church were put at its disposal and it became active under the name of EOKA on 1 April 1955.

EOKA stands for 'National organisation for the Cyprus struggle'. The word 'national', when used by Greek Cypriot leaders, means 'Hellenic' and 'pro-Enosis', as opposed to 'Cypriot' and 'pro-independence', a distinction which foreigners fail to grasp. EOKA's ranks were closed to Turkish Cypriots and to members of AKEL, the Greek Cypriot Communist Party. Turkish Cypriots were 'the religious and national enemy' who opposed Enosis.[5] EOKA bulletins informed Greek Cypriots that the 'holy fight' for union with Greece had begun. Anyone who opposed it would be treated as a 'traitor' and eliminated; all members of AKEL were traitors. The anticipated struggle with the Turkish Cypriots was to be delayed until the expulsion of the British from Cyprus, and in any case it was expected to be short and sharp. In the meantime Greek Cypriots were advised to avoid any kind of co-operation with Turkish Cypriots.

As bombs began to explode and people (British, Greek and Turkish) began to be shot in the back, the Turkish community organised its own underground resistance to EOKA. The following years, until the end of 1958, were marked by intercommunal and inter-Greek violence which, by the summer of 1958, had assumed all the characteristics of a civil war. During this period Greece, as the champion of EOKA, and Turkey, supporting the Turkish Cypriot resistance, came to the brink of war several times; while each year the Cyprus problem came before the UN General Assembly at the request of Greece. However, the General Assembly would not accept the Greek demands for the application of the principle of self-determination for Cyprus on a basis which would have ignored the rights and wishes of Turkish Cypriots and opened the way to Enosis. And it urged that the issue should be resolved through peaceful negotiations between the interested parties.

Later the Greek Cypriot leaders renamed the 'EOKA terror campaign', a 'struggle for independence' and accused the Turkish community of siding with the colonial power and opposing their freedom fighters, that is to say the EOKA terrorists. This was a deliberate distortion of both EOKA's purpose and the Turkish community's attitude. The Greek Cypriots were not struggling for 'independence' but for the union of Cyprus with Greece and this was the primary aim of EOKA. For the Turkish community Enosis was tantamount to slavery of the worst kind.

During the EOKA revolt, from 1955 to 1958, the Turkish community was in a very vulnerable position. Throughout the island Turkish Cypriots became a target for EOKA terrorists. Hundreds of Turkish Cypriots were killed and wounded while 6,000 Turkish Cypriot refugees, whose homes and properties in thirty-three villages had been destroyed by EOKA, looked to the future with grave suspicion. As the only hope of survival for the Turkish Cypriots lay in the defeat of EOKA which symbolised Greek colonisation, they had no choice but to defend themselves from EOKA attacks.

In the end, paradoxically, it was the Turkish Cypriots' resistance to Enosis which brought independence to the island and the establishment of a republic based on partnership between the two communities.

6   *The Birth of Independence*

In 1959, Turkey, Greece and Great Britain agreed on a formula for settling the Cyprus problem. It was obvious that Enosis was out of the question as long as Turkish Cypriots refused to accept it and Turkey supported them. A compromise proposition for 'double-Enosis' had been turned down by the Greek side, so the only remaining solution seemed to be 'independence'. After full consultations with the leaders of the two communities, the Zurich and London Agreements were drawn up. The two national communities were to become co-founder partners of the republic; Enosis in any form was to be prohibited and guaranteed against; the two communities were to be autonomous in their communal affairs, while participating in the central government on an agreed basis of 7:3. A functional federation was thus established by the two communities who worked together for eighteen months in preparing the Cyprus Constitution. Archbishop Makarios became the first President of this bi-national republic. His first executive action was to appoint Polycarpos Yorgadjis, a notorious EOKA killer with a pathological hatred for Turks, as Minister of the Interior. Subsequently other EOKA leaders were also given key positions in the government.

7 The Attempt to Destroy Independence

It soon became clear that Archbishop Makarios had never intended to promote and support the bi-national state.[6] He looked upon it as a Greek state and ignored virtually all Turkish rights enshrined in the constitution. He made no secret of his intention to amend the constitution at all costs and to abrogate the international Agreements which prohibited union with Greece. To this end he authorised the formation of underground armies to carry out a planned programme of action known as the Akritas Plan (see Appendix 11).

On 30 November 1963, Makarios confronted the Turkish wing of the Cyprus government with a proposal for thirteen amendments which he must have known in advance would not be accepted. He relied on the Turkish resistance to any changes in the constitution which had not yet been fully implemented because of the Greek Cypriots and which had only been in force for three years. For their part, the Turks were fully aware of the real intention behind the proposal. They had been following Makarios's increasingly strident statements about Enosis since independence. For example, on 5 September 1963 Makarios had said to a correspondent of *Uusi Suomi* of Stockholm: 'It is true that the goal of our struggle is to annex Cyprus to Greece.' In any case, the Turks had been put on their guard by a public speech of Makarios, barely a month before the declaration of independence, during which he said:

> The Agreements do not form the goal, they are the present and not the future. The Greek Cypriot people will continue their national cause and shape their future in accordance with their will. The Zurich and London Agreements have a number of positive elements but also negative ones, and the Greeks will work to take advantage of the positive elements and get rid of the negative ones. (Reported in the local Greek press on 28 July 1960)

The negative elements Makarios referred to were, of course, the right and the status which the Agreement gave to Turkish Cypriots and the provision which barred Enosis.

On 21 December 1963, Archbishop Makarios unleashed his secretly formed armed forces against the Turkish community.[7] Greece was hand in glove with the archbishop in this new conspiracy to destroy the Republic of Cyprus.[8] Within a few days a wave of violence spread throughout the island. Armed Greek Cypriot bands, assisted by the Greek Cypriot members of the Cypriot *gendarmerie* and police, attacked Turkish Cypriot homes in villages and towns in a ruthless rampage of murder and vandalism. Turkish Cypriots put up a stiff and effective resistance but, in the process, they suffered heavy loss of life and property. Archbishop Makarios declared that the Cyprus Agreements were no longer valid,[9] and by force of arms he ejected all Turkish Cypriot elements from the administration including the Vice-President of Cyprus and the three Turkish Cypriot ministers whose offices were broken into and ransacked.

Turkey, as a guarantor power, appealed to Greece and Great Britain – the other two guarantors – to join her in a concerted effort to end the bloodbath in the island. Greece, being deeply involved in the Greek Cypriot leaders' plot aimed at destroying the bi-communality of the state and abrogating the Agreements which had created that state, refused to help. Great Britain, with her large British colony in predominantly Greek areas and her military bases at stake, did not wish to intervene. Turkey, therefore, had to act alone to save the republic and the Turkish community from complete destruction. She sent two jet planes in a warning flight over Nicosia, whereupon Archbishop Makarios agreed to a 'ceasefire' under the supervision of a British peace force and to participate in a conference with the guarantors and representatives of the Greek and Turkish Cypriot communities to settle the crisis.

The conference was held in London on 15 January 1964. No positive result emerged from it because the Greek side insisted on a revision of the constitution and the Agreements in a way that would have left the Turkish community entirely at the mercy of the Greeks and leave the door wide open to Enosis. The attitude of the Greek delegates, no less than their unreasonable demands, contributed to the failure of the conference. They denied that there had been any pre-planned attacks on the Turkish community and accused Turkish Cypriots of deliberately creating the intercommunal troubles in order to partition the island. The Turkish Cypriot delegates who had just lived through terrible days and been confronted with the very real possibility of imminent death, realised that the Greek side, quite content with the *fait accompli* achieved through the use of arms and violence, would never recognise or restore their rights.

After the failure of the London Conference, the situation in the island further deteriorated with continuous Greek attacks on Turks throughout the island. The British peace force, which was also attacked and ridiculed by Greek Cypriot gunmen, could no longer cope with the task on its own and Great Britain brought the issue before the UN Security Council in mid-February 1964.

Having been spared a Turkish intervention through his acceptance of a ceasefire, Archbishop Makarios began to implement his plan to prove to the world that the 1960 Agreements which gave Turkey the right to intervene contradicted the principle of sovereignty. Whenever there was renewed fighting in Cyprus, and Turkey prepared to intervene and put an end to the massacres of Turks once and for all, Makarios would loudly protest about outside interference in the internal affairs of Cyprus.

8 Enter the UN Peace Force

On 4 March 1964, the UN Security Council adopted a resolution which provided for the dispatch of a Peace-Keeping Force to Cyprus, 'to use its best effort to prevent a recurrence of fighting and, as necessary, to contribute to the maintenance and restoration of law and order and a return to normal conditions'.

The arrival of the UN Peace-Keeping Force (UNFICYP) did not prevent the Greek Cypriot armed elements under the control of Makarios from attacking and oppressing Turkish Cypriots throughout the island. While Turkish Cypriots looked to the Security Council and UNFICYP for security and justice, the Greek Cypriot leaders maintained that 'peace and normality' could only be achieved if the UN Force helped Greek armed elements to deal with the Turkish Cypriot 'rebels'. Greece naturally propagated the same view. When Turkey remonstrated at the continued atrocities against Turkish Cypriots, Greece echoed the Greek Cypriot leaders' protest against outside interference.

9 *The Greek Occupation Army*

According to Greece, the elimination of Turks from Cyprus was an internal affair for Makarios, and Turkey had no right to come to their help. But, in the meantime, Greece herself was moving in. A few months after the arrival of UNFICYP more than 15,000 Greek troops were smuggled into the island under the guise of tourists and students. At a luncheon party given in honour of the visiting Greek Minister of Defence on 27 October 1964 Makarios declared:

> Greece has come to Cyprus, and Cyprus is Greece. I firmly believe that the Pan-Hellenic struggle for the union of Cyprus with motherland Greece will shortly be crowned with success. This success will be the beginning of a new era of Greek grandeur and glory.[10]

The UN Secretary-General's report at the end of the first three months of UNFICYP's operation in Cyprus presents a grim picture of the life of Turkish Cypriots in those days. Subsequent reports, submitted at three-monthly, and later six-monthly, intervals, show no improvement. Greek troops continued to be brought in and effectively became an 'occupation army'. A Greek Cypriot armed force – National Guard – was established under the command of Greek General Staff in complete contravention of the constitution. This force later mounted many attacks jointly with Greek troops and under Greek army officers on Turkish Cypriot enclaves. These troops were equipped with arms imported secretly from Greece and also from Czechoslovakia. The Greek Cypriot personnel swore allegiance to Greece, and Greece openly declared Cyprus to be 'within the Greek Defence Area'.

UNFICYP was able to prevent minor clashes and de-escalate many local incidents, but it was never able to prevent determined and pre-planned attacks on isolated Turkish villages and enclaves. Even members of the UN Force were attacked during such operations. But its usefulness as an 'international eyewitness' was by no means negligible for it deterred the Greek Cypriots from committing greater atrocities.

10　*The UN Mediation Effort*

A UN 'mediation' initiative, in pursuance of the 4 March 1964 resolution, was first assigned to Ambassador Sakari Tuomioja. But after Mr Tuomioja's sudden death, Mr Galo Plaza was designated to complete the mission, on 16 September 1964. After consulting all the parties involved, Mr Plaza submitted his report to the UN Secretary-General on 26 March 1965 and it was published as Security Council document S/6253 on the same date. But the mediation effort went no further. The Greek Cypriot leaders, claiming to be the 'government of Cyprus', were very angry with Galo Plaza because he had ruled out self-determination and Enosis. Turkish Cypriots, on the other hand, considered the Galo Plaza report pro-Greek. Turkey concluded, justifiably in the circumstances, that through the publication of this report Galo Plaza had irretrievably damaged his role as a mediator and had set out to become a pro-Greek arbitrator. Thus the Plaza report failed to contribute to a settlement of the Cyprus problem. There was disagreement between the interested parties on the question of a successor to Galo Plaza and the mediation effort petered out.[11]

11 *The Turkish Cypriot Administration*

The Turkish Cypriot community, which had been forcibly ejected from all governmental functions and put beyond the protection of the constitution from the outset of the inter-communal troubles in December 1963, was also deprived of all essential public services and all forms of legal benefits from state sources. In fact, the Turkish community was forced into an economic and administrative vacuum. Existence in a vacuum is impossible and the Turkish Cypriots therefore mustered all their available potential and organised themselves within the limits of the 1960 constitution. At first a 'general committee', headed by the Vice-President and comprising the three Turkish Cypriot ministers of the republic, was formed. The committee was served by the Turkish Cypriot civil servants who were prevented, by force of arms, from attending their work in the Greek sector.[12]

The Turkish Cypriots' initiative was presented to the world by the Greek Cypriot leaders as a 'defection' from the government for the purposes of partitioning the island. This was a deliberate lie, for the Turkish Cypriot civil servants could not go to their places of work on the Greek side for fear of being shot on sight by Greek Cypriot armed bands. A number of Turkish Cypriot civil servants who had ventured out to go to their offices were abducted and never seen again.

At first the situation appealed to the Greek Cypriot leaders because it served their plan of eliminating the Turkish element from the government in preparation for the Hellenisation of the island. The bi-communal structure was an impediment which had to be removed from 'Greek Cyprus'. The Turkish Cypriots had either to accept minority rights or expect continued pressure from the Greek side.

However, the Greek Cypriot pressure merely resulted in the development and consolidation of the Turkish Cypriot administrative structure. Thus on 28 December 1967, after a massive attack by a combined Greek–Greek Cypriot force on the Turkish village of Kophinou in the Larnaca District, the 'Provisional Turkish Cypriot Administration' was established. The Basic Provisions of the new administration provided for the setting up of a legislature, composed of Turkish Cypriot members of the House of Representatives and the Communal Chamber, and an Executive Council, to exercise administrative power in the Turkish Cypriot areas. Section 1 of the Basic Provisions set out the reason for the establishment of the administration and its objective. This stated that 'until all the provisions of the 1960 constitution were applied, all Turks living in Turkish areas should be attached to this administration'.

This new arrangement, which constituted an evolutionary organic development in the field of Cypriot constitutional law, illustrates the way in which the Turkish Cypriot administration took over or assumed its share of functions under the 1960 constitution, thus showing its intention to give a constructive hand in reshaping the 1960 bi-communal partnership.[13]

As the prospects for the restoration of the 1960 constitution receded, the word 'provisional' was dropped and the Turkish Cypriot Administration continued to function as a fully fledged government catering for all the needs of the Turkish community and sustaining its resistance to Greek

35

Cypriot aggression. Nevertheless the Turkish Cypriots were still surrounded by hostile armed Greek elements and lived as defiant hostages in their own country until they were liberated by the Turkish Peace Force in July 1974.[14]

12 *Oppression and Violence*

The atrocities committed by the Greek Cypriot leadership under Archbishop Makarios shocked the civilised world. The island was visited by hundreds of foreign correspondents who reported the brutalities committed against the Turkish Cypriots and the appalling conditions under which they lived (see Appendix 2). The UN Secretary-General described these conditions to the Security Council in his report dated 10 September 1964 (S/5950) as follows:

189. Ever since the outbreak of violence on 21 December 1963, a variety of restrictions . . . have been imposed upon the Turkish Cypriots. The isolation of the Turkish Cypriot Community, due to the restrictions placed on their movement on the roads, brought hardship on the members of the community as well as serious disruption of their economic activities. . . . 190. In addition to losses incurred in agriculture and in industry during the first part of the year, the Turkish Community had lost other sources of its income including the salaries of over 4,000 persons who were employed by the Cyprus Government and by public and private concerns located in the Greek Cypriot zones. The trade of the Turkish Community had considerably declined during the period, due to the existing situation, and unemployment reached a very high level as approximately 25,000 Turkish Cypriots had become refugees. Expenditure of the Turkish Communal Chamber on

development and other projects, as well as other expenditure, had dropped considerably as a yearly subsidy formerly received from the Government had ceased to be granted in 1964[15] . . . approximately half the population came to be on relief. In accordance with figures published by the Turkish Cypriot Communal Chamber, the number of persons receiving some kind of assistance from the Red Crescent relief amounted to about 56,000, including 25,000 displaced persons, 23,500 unemployed and 7,500 dependants of missing persons, disabled and others.

The same report records that

179. In refugee camps near Nicosia many hundreds of children living in crowded temporary quarters and exposed during the great heat of the summer months to the risk of dehydration survived without serious illness partly because an UNFICYP architect and military engineers planned and, with local help, built provisional matting roofs to give shelter from sun as well as open-air showers.

180. UNFICYP carried out a detailed survey of all damage to properties throughout the island during the disturbances, including the Tylliria fighting. It shows that in 109 villages, most of them Turkish Cypriot or mixed villages, 527 houses have been destroyed while 2,000 others have suffered damage from looting. In Ktima 38 houses and shops have been destroyed totally and 122 partially. In the Omorphita suburb of Nicosia 50 houses have been totally destroyed while a further 240 have been partially destroyed there and in adjacent suburbs. In many Turkish villages, crowded by the arrival of displaced persons, there is an acute shortage of medical facilities.

The UN Secretary-General went on to report that on

receiving complaints from Turkish Cypriots that they were being starved, UNFICYP carried out a preliminary survey on 16 August 1964 and found that 40 per cent of the villages had no flour and 25 per cent of the villages had flour for only one or two weeks. The need for milk and dairy products, rice and salt was acute, while kerosene was in extremely limited supply. Medical attention in villages was notably lacking. In the cities, although the situation was better than in the villages, it was deteriorating rapidly. The UN Secretary-General also records that despite strong representations by UNFICYP, and an agreement by the Greek Cypriot authorities to ease the restrictions, Red Crescent relief supply convoys were held up by Greek Cypriot forces and more sectors were put on the list of restricted areas by the Greek Cypriot authorities.

The Greek Cypriot leaders adopted a new tactic to hoodwink the UN. They eased off their pressure on the Turkish community a few weeks before the Security Council debates on Cyprus to win some favourable comment in the UN Secretary-General's report, but thereafter they resumed their attacks with fresh vigour. These tactics of on-and-off pressure, which the Greek Cypriot leaders hoped would ultimately wear out the Turks, continued until mid-November 1967. By this time, the Turkish Cypriots had lost 103 villages where their homes had been looted and destroyed, their lands laid waste or used by Greek Cypriots without any payment and their flocks, agricultural implements, tractors, lorries and cars taken over by the Greeks. The toll in life and limb was equally great. Five hundred Turkish Cypriots (including women and children) had been killed and more than 1,000 wounded and maimed. Another 203 were missing.

The indiscriminate killing of Turks was seen by independent observers, as well as by the Turkish Cypriots themselves, as part of a policy of genocide. A report in the

Washington Post on 17 February 1964, for example, said: 'Greek Cypriot fanatics appear bent on a policy of genocide.' In the mixed village of Ayios Vassilios, north-west of Nicosia, the bodies of twenty-one Turks were exhumed from a mass grave in the presence of British soldiers and members of the St John Ambulance Association on 13 January 1964. Some of the bodies were bound in positions which indicated that the victims had been tortured before they were massacred.

The wave of vandalism did not even spare holy places. Every mosque, shrine and place of prayer in areas overrun by Greek Cypriot armed bands was desecrated and destroyed. This demonstrated the Greek Cypriots' hatred of Turkish Cypriots, not only as 'Turks' but also as 'Moslems'. The religious aspect of the Cyprus conflict has been overlooked or diminished by foreign observers, but Archbishop Makarios is on record as declaring that 'the struggle of Greek Cypriots is not only for the motherland [Greece] but also for the faith.[16]

13 Turkish Cypriot Refugees

More than 25,000 Turkish Cypriots, who had fled from their homes as a result of armed attacks, had to live in hastily constructed camps or in slums which lacked even the most basic amenities. The Greek Cypriot leaders callously described the flight of these refugees to safety as an organised exodus to partition the island. This was a lie and was exposed as such by the UN Secretary-General's reports. In his report S/8286 of 8 December 1967, the Secretary-General stated:

> 126. When the disturbances broke out in December 1963 and continued in the first part of 1964, thousands of Turkish Cypriots fled from their homes, taking with them only what they could drive or carry, and sought refuge in what they considered to be safer Turkish Cypriot villages and areas.
>
> The refusal of the Greek Cypriot authorities to allow the Turkish Cypriot refugees to return to their homes in conditions of safety, effectively frustrated persistent Turkish efforts to rehabilitate them. They also obstructed attempts to improve their living conditions.

In his report S/7001 of 10 December 1965, the UN Secretary-General said:

> 73. Another factor which has tended to aggravate the

refugee problem has been the National Guard policy of asserting government authority by establishing a military presence in Turkish Cypriot areas.

In the same report the Secretary-General reveals that in September 1965 the President of the Turkish Communal Chamber sought UNFICYP assistance in the partial removal of the Greek restriction on the import of building materials to allow an improvement scheme to be carried out in the uncomfortable and unhygienic refugee settlements, but the Greek Cypriot authorities would not approve the release of building materials even for the refugees.

The Greek Cypriot leaders talked constantly about the necessity of rehabilitating the Turkish refugees and promised to provide financial aid for that purpose, but in fact they used every device to discourage or prevent the refugees' return to their homes. A festering refugee problem for the Turkish Cypriot administration was in the political interests of the Greek Cypriot leadership. An international research report on Cyprus pointed out that 'the world at large, in general, paid little attention to the plight of Turkish refugees and gave them little in the way of sympathy or support'.[17] The whole burden of the Turkish Cypriot refugees, amounting to no less than £1 million (sterling) a year (about US $2 million) was borne by Turkey and the Turkish Red Crescent Society for eleven years from 1963 to 1974.

14 *Missing Turkish Cypriots*

The Greek Cypriot armed bands and the so-called security forces of the Makarios administration started taking hostages from the very beginning of the armed conflict a few days before Christmas 1963. Within a few days some 700 Turkish Cypriots, mostly women and children, were carried away as hostages from Turkish areas in Nicosia. The Greek Cypriots explained that they had 'evacuated' 500 Turkish women and children from the danger areas. A number of these hostages were later murdered.[18]

When the Turkish Cypriots also began taking hostages in retaliation, the Greeks agreed to an exchange of hostages. The exchange was effected on 30–31 December 1963 under the supervision of Duncan Sandys, the British Secretary for Commonwealth Relations, who was in Cyprus at the time. Fifty-four Turkish Cypriots were exchanged for twenty-six Greek Cypriots.

As the Greek attacks and raids continued, more Turkish Cypriots were taken as hostages from their homes, on the main roads and at roadblocks. In one case, a senior Turkish employee of Barclays Bank was taken away at gun-point from his office at the Famagusta branch of the bank in broad daylight. He was never seen again. The Greek Cypriot authorities did not admit any hostages had been taken, so the Turks listed them as missing persons and informed UNFICYP.

All efforts to trace the missing Turkish Cypriots failed.

In his report no. S/6228 of 11 March 1965, the UN Secretary-General made the following observation:

> 117. Figures supplied by the Turkish Cypriot Missing Persons Bureau as at 1 March 1965 show that 209 Turkish Cypriots are still missing. This figure is the same as that given in the last report (S/6102, 93–94). Efforts to trace these persons by ICRC and UNFICYP have been without result and there is little prospect of finding them alive.

Further exhaustive inquiries by the Turkish Cypriot authorities ended all hope of finding the missing Turks alive. Years later the Greek Cypriot authorities officially stated that none of the missing Turkish Cypriots was being held as a captive or prisoner on the Greek side. In the circumstances, one can reasonably assume that the missing Turks had been murdered in cold blood by their abductors.

The pattern of abduction and of mass murder which had continued relentlessly until 1968 reached its peak in July 1974 during and after the coup. In the two months after the Turkish intervention nearly 800 Turkish Cypriots disappeared. Later about 200 of them were found by UNFICYP in mass graves in Aloa, Sandallaris and Maratha. Eighty-four young men from the villages of Mari, Zyyi and Tokhni who were taken away 'for questioning' were lined up and shot. Greek Cypriots refused a request by UNFICYP to open up the common grave where, according to eyewitness accounts, the young Turks had been buried. At Alaminyo fifteen more Turkish Cypriots had been executed.

15 *Economic Pressures and Blockades*

After ousting the Turkish element from the government structure, the Greek Cypriot leaders concentrated their efforts on consolidating their *de facto* administration as the 'government of Cyprus'. Although the Greek Cypriot administration, as such, bore no resemblance to the 1960 constitutional pattern of a bi-communal government, the UN and other international bodies, as a matter of political convenience, treated this administration as if it were the government for the whole of Cyprus. Turkish Cypriots refused to accept this unconstitutional state of affairs and defied the Greek Cypriot administration at all levels. Archbishop Makarios had no authority whatsoever in Turkish Cypriot areas from 1963 to 1974.

Encouraged by the recognition of their administration as 'the government', the Greek Cypriots increased their economic and administrative pressure on the Turkish community. The Greek Cypriot authorities devised various restrictive practices under the pretext of 'lawful necessity' to force the Turkish Cypriot community to submit to their illegal and arbitrary rule. The salaries and emoluments of Turkish Cypriot civil servants and government employees were withheld; the social insurance benefits of old-age pensioners, widows and orphans were stopped; the grants and subsidies, provided for by the constitution, were suspended; all kinds of

45

communication services (internal and external) were denied; the registration of newly born babies was refused and students studying abroad were not allowed to return to the island.

Movement between Turkish areas, through Greek-controlled roads, was subject to degrading searches and long delays at roadblocks. The Greek authorities would place the Turkish areas under a total blockade whenever they liked, preventing the entry even of medicine and essential food supplies into the area put out of bounds.

The UN Secretary-General informed the Security Council of the Turkish community's plight in his report no. S/6426 of 10 June 1965. He said:

> 104. The Turkish Cypriot population has continued to be subject to hardships of various kinds, some of them enormous. These include restrictions on the freedom of movement of civilians, economic restrictions, the unavailability of some essential public services, and the sufferings of refugees . . .

The UN Secretary-General urged the Greek Cypriot administration to relax restrictions imposed on the Turkish community but obtained no results. Eighteen months later he made the following observation in his report no. S/7611 of 8 December 1966:

> 122. Economically isolated, the Turkish Cypriot Community has found itself in a backwater as far as trade, industry and employment are concerned, and does not participate in the economic expansion of the country or the development of its resources. Many of the estimated 20,000 refugees and displaced persons in the Turkish Cypriot enclaves are unemployed, and their enforced idleness emphasises the isolation of the community,

whose economy is sustained by financial assistance and relief supplies from Turkey . . . about one-third of the Turkish Cypriot population is estimated to need some form of welfare relief.

As there was no serious reaction from the Security Council to the gross violation of human rights and injustices exposed in the UN Secretary-General's reports, the Greek Cypriots left their Turkish 'victims' to suffer in their beleaguered areas and continued to develop Greek areas through international aid and credits.

16 *Profit from Conflict*

One of the strange paradoxes of the Cyprus problem is that the Greek Cypriots benefited financially from their failure to resolve the intercommunal conflict. To begin with, a quarter of the population of the island, the entire Turkish community had been eliminated from the state budget. This alone saved the Greek Cypriots at least Cyprus £6–8 million (about US $12–16 million) a year. The financial aid from Turkey for Turkish Cypriots, which amounted to about 13 million pounds sterling a year (about 26 million US dollars) had to be transferred through the Greek-controlled Central Bank of Cyprus and this resulted in a substantial 'hard currency' gain for the Greek Cypriot treasury. The Central Bank paid the Turkish Cypriots in Cyprus pounds, all of which was spent in the Greek Cypriot market because all ports were in Greek hands and no other market was available for the Turks. The Greek Cypriots also pocketed virtually all of the money spent by UNFICYP in Cyprus. That is why Archbishop Makarios described the UN Peace-Keeping Force as his 'permanent tourists'!

By 1970 there was a real boom in Greek Cypriot trade and industry, particularly in the field of tourism. Greek Cypriot propaganda had been successful in projecting the island as a land of peace and opportunity. 'Turkish Cypriots are just a nuisance and time will solve that problem', they said. So, tourists and foreign capital poured into the Greek sectors. Tourists coming to the island, who were not allowed to cross into the Turkish sectors or to know what was happening to a quarter of the population of the island, believed Cyprus was still a fun-in-the-sun island. Life for the Turkish Cypriots was no fun at all, but a continuous struggle for survival. Their only hope lay in Turkey. The Greek Cypriot leaders knew this and they made every effort to demoralise the Turkish Cypriots and to shatter their hopes.[19]

17 *The Kophinou Attack*

In mid-November 1967 the notorious terrorist leader, General
Grivas, who had been appointed Supreme Commander of
the Greek and Greek Cypriot armed forces by Archbishop
Makarios, launched an attack on the Turkish village of
Kophinou and the Turkish inhabitants of the neighbouring
village of Ayios Theodoros in the Larnaca District. The
operation was ferocious in its intensity and effect. Within a
few hours twenty-eight Turks were murdered and scores
wounded. Turkish homes were ransacked and deliberately
set on fire. Some of the wounded had kerosene poured over
them and were then set on fire.

The timing of the Kophinou attack is very significant. The
Greco-Turkish dialogue on Cyprus, which had started in
May 1965 and continued after the military takeover in
Greece in April 1967, had just come to an abrupt end as a
result of the insistence of the Greek Prime Minister on Enosis
at a meeting with the Turkish Prime Minister at Keshan on
9–10 September 1967. Archbishop Makarios had persuaded
the military leaders in Athens that championing the Enosis
cause would win them considerable public support in
Greece and among Greek Cypriots in Cyprus. A few
months earlier the Greek Cypriot House of Representatives
Journal of 27 June 1967 reported that, on 26 June, the
deputies had unanimously passed a resolution declaring that
the struggle for Enosis would continue until the union of
Cyprus with the motherland, Greece, was achieved:

Interpreting the age-long aspirations of the Greeks of Cyprus, the House declares that despite any adverse circumstances it will not suspend the struggle being conducted with the support of all Greeks, until this struggle ends in success through the union of the whole and undivided Cyprus with the motherland, without any intermediary stage.

The Kophinou attack was, therefore, planned to demonstrate the fiery spirit of the Enosis struggle and to prove to Turkish Cypriots that Turkey could do nothing about it.

In his report no. S/8286 of 8 December 1967 (para. 48), the UN Secretary-General stated that the Kophinou operation had 'caused heavy loss of life and had grave repercussions'.[20] The brutalities committed during the Kophinou attack immediately provoked a very strong reaction from Turkey. An ultimatum to Greece demanded that the attack should cease immediately and a task force was held in readiness to go to Cyprus in case hostilities continued. Turkey and Greece were thus brought to the brink of war yet again. To avert a physical intervention by Turkey, which was fully justified in the circumstances, President Johnson sent his special envoy, Mr Cyrus Vance, to Cyprus. Shuttling between Turkey, Greece and Cyprus, Mr Vance succeeded in defusing the crisis. He secured an agreement whereby Greece agreed to withdraw her forces (whose number, according to Turkish Cypriot intelligence reports, had reached 20,000 over the years) together with George Grivas. Furthermore, the Greek Cypriot administration undertook to compensate the Turkish inhabitants of the two villages.

However, it was discovered later that the withdrawal of the Greek troops had been only partially carried out and that several thousand mainland Greek troops and officers continued to be attached to the Greek Cypriot National Guard. When the UN took up this question with the

51

Greek Cypriot leaders, the latter explained that these officers and men were on contract to train the Greek Cypriot National Guard, itself an unconstitutional force, and therefore were not covered by the withdrawal agreement. It is ironic that it was these 'instructors' who were to stage a successful coup against Archbishop Makarios in 1974. Needless to say, Archbishop Makarios also went back on his promise to compensate the Turkish Cypriot victims of the Kophinou attack.

18 *Exploratory Talks*

A positive outcome of the Kophinou crisis was the introduction of direct talks between the two communities. From 1964 until November 1967, Archbishop Makarios had consistently refused to meet the Turkish Cypriot leaders unless they agreed to discuss minority rights within a Greek Cyprus. Now, under pressure from the UN, the USA and Great Britain, the archbishop agreed to have 'unofficial, exploratory talks' with representatives of the Turkish community.

In the meantime, Archbishop Makarios decided to remove the barricades and roadblocks surrounding the Turkish areas. He had now consolidated his military position and could afford to relax. Turkish Cypriots who travelled on the roads would, in any case, have to submit to Greek Cypriot police and military control. Even Turkish Cypriot members of the Cyprus police force were confined to Turkish areas and could not travel on the roads under Greek control. The freedom of movement which the archbishop appeared to have so generously granted to the Turks was, in effect, an extension of his unconstitutional rule over them.

The UN urged the Turkish side to reciprocate. The Turkish Cypriot administration expressed their willingness to do so, provided that the Greek Cypriots travelling through Turkish Cypriot areas would agree to abide by local regulations in exactly the same way that Turkish Cypriots were expected to do when travelling in Greek areas. The Greeks rejected the offer as unacceptable. They would

53

not recognise any rule or authority on the Turkish side.

The intercommunal talks began between myself and Mr Glafcos Clerides in Beirut on 6 June 1968, and were transferred to Nicosia a week later.

The Greek Cypriots' excuse for their uprising in December 1963 was the amendment of the constitution, therefore the talks began with proposals for such an amendment. The Turkish Cypriots, who lived in enclaves surrounded by the Greeks, were subjected to every kind of pressure and needed peace and an early return to normality. Therefore, they agreed to most of the Greek demands and indicated their willingness to discuss the rest.

The Turkish Cypriot concessions were very substantial in the circumstances which prevailed at the time. In return for these concessions the Turkish Cypriot side wanted any future agreement to continue to guarantee Cyprus against Enosis or union with any other country, and 'local autonomy' to be the basis for a final settlement in recognition of the partnership status of the Turkish community.

The Greek Cypriot side, which appeared determined not to sign an agreement barring Enosis,[21] argued that the question of 'a guarantee' was a matter to be discussed by all the signatories of the 1960 Agreements after the settlement of the constitutional issues. Although there was a wide degree of agreement on the 'functions' of the local authorities and on the principle of 'local autonomy', when the issue came up for consideration and decision the Greek Cypriot side was reluctant to give any meaningful autonomy to the Turks. The sort of autonomy envisaged by the Greeks was similar to the powers delegated to 'village commissions' and 'improvement boards' by the British administration.

For over two years the talks dragged on with fruitless exchanges of views on the issues of the legislature, the judiciary, the police and local autonomy. There were other important constitutional matters still awaiting discussion such as the question of compensation, the unpaid salaries of the Turkish civil servants and government employees, and the constitutional grant for education. The Turkish side drew up a comprehensive list of such matters which needed consideration. The Turks expected that an agreement on non-political issues would enhance the chances of success in the intercommunal talks.

The answer to the Turkish Cypriots' expectations came from Archbishop Makarios himself on 14 March 1971 when, at a public gathering at the village of Yialousa, the archbishop made the declaration quoted in the Introduction to this book:

Cyprus is Greek. Cyprus has been Greek since the dawn of history and it will remain Greek. Greek and undivided we have taken it over, Greek and undivided we shall preserve it. Greek and undivided we shall deliver it to Greece.[22]

Makarios's declaration of intent – to deliver Cyprus to Greece – at a time when his representative in the intercommunal talks was ostensibly negotiating for a solution based on independence was a very serious matter. The Turkish side officially asked for a clarification of Greek Cypriot policy in the light of Archbishop Makarios's Yialousa declaration. No satisfactory answer was given and so the talks broke down after a last meeting on 20 September 1971.

19 *Expanded Talks*

The UN Secretary-General made strenuous efforts to re-activate the talks. In an *aide-mémoire* dated 18 October 1971 and circulated to all the parties concerned, he suggested that the intercommunal talks should be resumed in an expanded form, with the participation of his Special Representative in Cyprus and of two constitutional experts – one representing Turkey and the other Greece.[23]

The formula was accepted, but the resumption of the talks was delayed when it was discovered early in February 1972 that Archbishop Makarios had secretly imported a substantial quantity of arms and ammunition of Czech origin into the island.[24] The expanded talks eventually began on 8 June 1972. At the inaugural meeting the following statement (reported in the Turkish Cypriot press of 9 June 1972) was made on behalf of the Turkish Cypriot side:

> The area in which Cyprus is located is highly sensitive; the inseparable ties of the two communities with their respective motherlands are too strong to be denied. The fact that whatever happens between the two communities is inevitably reflected in Ankara and Athens cannot be disregarded. We, therefore, as the two national communities in Cyprus, the co-founders of the independence and sovereignty of Cyprus, and partners in the administrative set-up of the Cyprus State, have a duty not only to our respective communities and to Cyprus as a whole, but also have an international duty maintaining the peace in

this delicate area in the knowledge that, by doing so, we help our respective motherlands to normalise their political relations. Cyprus should be and can be made a bridge of Greco-Turkish friendship and co-operation. Our role to this end can be most significant. We want peace and justice in the light of established rights and political status.

While the expanded talks went on, in spasmodic fashion, Archbishop Makarios continued to make provocative Enosis speeches in various parts of the island. The local Greek press ridiculed the Turkish Cypriots' stand on partnership rights and their demand for local autonomy. They urged that the Greek Cypriots' right to self-determination should never be curtailed for the sake of Turkish Cypriots who were free to leave the island if they did not like living under Greek rule.

Despite the hostile comments of the local Greek press and the negative attitude of the Greek Cypriot political parties, who characterised the Turkish Cypriots' insistence on local autonomy as 'excessive demands', the talks continued.

On 2 April 1974 the Greek Cypriot negotiator, Mr Clerides, walked out of a meeting because the Turkish Premier, Mr Ecevit, was reported to have declared that 'a federal system of government was the best solution for Cyprus'. Later, I told reporters that I had clearly reaffirmed the unchanged Turkish Cypriot stand on local autonomy in an independent Cyprus to the satisfaction of everyone at the meeting, except Mr Clerides. Despite Mr Ecevit's assurances that there was no change in the Turkish position with regard to the intercommunal talks, Mr Clerides did not return to the negotiating table. It was obvious that the Greek side was using Mr Ecevit's remarks about a federal system of government as an excuse for breaking off the talks.

Through the efforts of the Turkish side and the perseverance of the UN Secretary-General, the talks were resumed on 11 June 1974 and the two sides exchanged documents outlining how the 1960 constitution would function within the order to be established. The basic difference between the two sides was the Greek Cypriots' insistence on a 'unitary state', which they clearly wished to use as a means of achieving Enosis. The Turkish Cypriots would not budge from their stand on 'regional autonomy' in a Cyprus guaranteed against Enosis. The last meeting took place on 9 July 1974 without achieving anything. Thus six years of negotiations were wasted because the Greek side was determined to impose its own solution.

The Greek responsibility for the failure of the talks during this period was later admitted by Mr Clerides. In a public statement in August 1978, he referred to a 'near agreement' during the intercommunal talks between 1971 and 1972. He claimed that he had recommended the acceptance of the agreement but the Greek Cypriot Council of Ministers had not shared his view.[25]

When the Kophinou crisis of 1967 was over, Archbishop Makarios had assured the UN Secretary-General that he had no intention of attacking the Turks again. But he continued to import arms for his army to prepare them for a future opportunity to strike against the Turkish Cypriots. The plan was to neutralise the Turkish Cypriots within a few hours, thus depriving Turkey of a chance to intervene. He believed that five years of harassment, economic restrictions and food blockades had considerably undermined the physical and moral fabric of the Turkish Cypriots' resistance. Therefore, he continued to deliver speeches in which he confidently predicted the achievement of Enosis in the near future and in the process undermined the intercommunal talks.

The prolongation of the Cyprus dispute gave the Greek Cypriot community an unprecedented economic prosperity and Archbishop Makarios an overweening self-confidence. It also led to a series of developments within the Greek Cypriot camp, which directly contributed to the archbishop's downfall in July 1974.

20 *Inter-Greek Violence*

Makarios's ostensible inactivity against the Turks was interpreted by his rivals in Cyprus and in Greece, including members of the church in both countries, as a deviation from the Enosis policy. Despite Makarios's repeated assurances that he was still loyal to his Enosis oath, the Greek camp became divided into hostile factions. The thinly veiled distrust between Makarios and the military rulers in Greece turned into open hostility. The Colonels were aware that Makarios was an ardent 'Royalist' and that he was furtively collaborating with those who wished to overthrow them. Makarios disliked the Colonels because they had readily bowed to Turkey's demand for the withdrawal of Greek troops from Cyprus after the ill-fated Kophinou operation. He never forgave the Colonels for their cowardly retreat and, for their part, the Colonels never forgave him for his brinkmanship which had ultimately forced them into a humiliating situation.

By April 1969 several underground groups had mushroomed in the Greek Cypriot sector to carry on the Enosis struggle. The most active of these groups was the 'National Front' which carried out daring raids on rural police stations, military camps and mines, stealing arms, ammunition and explosives. Official premises, trade union offices and homes of politicians became targets for bomb attacks. The 'National Front' urged

. . . the formation of specially trained shock-troops around

59

areas inhabited by Turkish Cypriots, so as to stall all possible danger from them. These units must be trained in such a way as to be able to occupy all of the main military positions of the Turkish Cypriot rebels with lightning speed at a given order. Their training must also include learning the Turkish language.[26]

The most dramatic incident in this period of violence was the shooting down of Archbishop Makarios's helicopter on 8 March 1970 during an attempted assassination. Makarios had a lucky escape but his pilot was seriously wounded by bullets fired at the helicopter from the terrace of a building in the vicinity of the archbishopric. There were other abortive attempts on his life. The Greek Cypriot Communists, who seemed to be well informed about the terrorist activities, claimed that these murderous attacks were instigated from Athens. However, Makarios remained passive to the point of complacency. Instead of dealing firmly with these underground organisations he tried to appease them. He appealed to them to dissolve themselves, and even granted an amnesty to convicted terrorists.[27]

Terrorism and anarchy in the Greek sector took a more serious turn after the secret landing in Cyprus of the ex-EOKA leader, General Grivas, in September 1971. Grivas had been withdrawn from the island by Greece after the Kophinou crisis in November 1967. Immediately after his landing, he went into hiding and began to reactivate EOKA in a new form as EOKA 'B'. Greek army officers in Cyprus helped him in his new organisation and ex-EOKA members who had had no favours from Makarios, offered their services to Grivas.

On 26 October 1971, Grivas issued a proclamation denouncing the Greek Cypriot leadership under Makarios as unworthy of the Greek community. He declared that he had come back to fulfil the age-long aspiration of the Greek community to unite Cyprus with Greece. (Grivas's proclamation was reported in all Greek Cypriot newspapers the following day.) Makarios replied three days later, disclosing that he had, from time to time, clearly and categorically told Greek governments that he would unhestitatingly proclaim Enosis, if they were prepared to accept Enosis and share the responsibilities for the repercussions from such a venture.[28]

Although Greece disclaimed responsibility for Grivas's secret landing in Cyprus, the Greek Cypriot leadership believed that he had been allowed to 'escape' to Cyprus in order to provide a check on Archbishop Makarios and his Communist friends. This view was also held by independent foreign observers.

At first Makarios tried to win Grivas to his side and offered him an important post in his Cabinet, but Grivas refused. Later, Makarios asked Grivas to join him in forging a new policy for the national struggle. The two men had a secret meeting in Nicosia. They agreed on their common goal, Enosis, but disagreed on how it should be achieved. Archbishop Makarios told Grivas that if his aim was Enosis 'then both I and the people of Cyprus are ready to enter such a struggle provided it is backed by the Greek government' (National Front papers). However, Grivas wanted an immediate military campaign, while Makarios insisted on caution and a low-geared approach. Above all, Archbishop Makarios did not want to bolster the prestige of the Colonels in Greece by uniting the island with Greece at that stage. He felt that he could afford to wait. So Grivas continued to organise more raids and bomb attacks, while Makarios went on assuring his community and foreign diplomats that he could eliminate Grivas and his armed gang any day he wanted. He declared Grivas to be an outlaw but never made any serious attempt to arrest him. In an interview with John Harrison of the London *Daily Express* on 6 April 1973 Archbishop Makarios said:

I would say that General Grivas is rather in direct control of the Enosis campaign. He is a good patriot and he would desire to see, as all Greek Cypriots would, Cyprus united with Greece.

Union of Cyprus with Greece has always been the national aspiration of the Greek Cypriots. This national feeling has deep roots and the Greek Cypriots would favour Enosis under any circumstances. Various factors, however, and mainly the opposition of Turkey do not make Enosis attainable.

Grivas died of a heart attack on 27 January 1974 at the house of one of his friends in Limasol where he was hiding.

It is relevant to mention here that during the Makarios–Grivas feud an erroneous impression had been given that Makarios was working for permanent independence through the intercommunal talks and that Grivas was trying to stop him. In fact both men were pursuing the same goal – Enosis – but had different ideas about how to achieve it. Mr Glafcos Clerides set the record straight in a declaration he made in the House of Representatives on 10 January 1971. Refuting an allegation that General Grivas had organised illegal armed groups so as to prevent a 'treacherous solution to the Cyprus problem', Mr Clerides said:

> Common sense ought to have led the General [Grivas] to the conclusion that the carrying out of talks for five years without arriving at a solution meant that the Greek Cypriot side did not attend them in order to arrive at 'any solution', or to make inadmissible concessions for an 'unnational solution' and that their bargaining at the talks was aimed at safeguarding the national interest in its true sense.

'National interest in its true sense', has only one meaning

for the Greek Cypriots, and that is Enosis. Mr Clerides was not openly demanding 'Enosis' in the talks but, as he admitted, he was striving for a solution that would not exclude its achievement. It was only natural that the Turkish Cypriot side should insist that Enosis be effectively barred in any new arrangement and that complete Greek Cypriot domination should be counter-blanced by an adequate degree of local autonomy which would enable the Turkish community to look after its own security affairs lest the tragedy of the past were to be repeated in the future.

21 *The Coup*

After the death of George Grivas, EOKA 'B' came under the direct control of the Junta in Athens. Terrorist activities in the Greek sector continued with the assistance and guidance of the Greek army officers. But now Makarios began to hit back with his Tactical Reserve Force which he had established to combat the terrorists. Within the following six months most of the local leaders were apprehended and a considerable quantity of secret documents seized which provided ample evidence proving the complicity of Greek officers in EOKA 'B' activities. Makarios finally showed defiance and asked the Junta to withdraw its officers from Cyprus (see Appendix 3).

In Greece the Junta was suffering from internal problems and the conflict with Makarios was, ultimately, to prove its undoing. In early July there were reports of a possible coup in Nicosia inspired by Athens, however Makarios's spokesman said that any such attempt would be defeated by strong popular resistance. The archbishop himself later stated that he had never believed that the Junta would attempt a coup in Cyprus because it would automatically have provoked a Turkish intervention.

Those who followed the events closely at the time realised that a power struggle had become inevitable between Makarios and the Junta and that one of the two would have to go. The Junta could not afford to lose and it seemed more likely that it would take desperate steps to protect itself.

The Greek Cypriot warning about a strong popular reaction to a coup was not heeded by Athens. The Junta struck in the early hours of 15 July 1974. Within a few hours the broadcasting station was seized, the presidential palace was razed to the ground by gunfire and Nicosia airport closed to traffic. The National Guard announced that they had seized power to prevent civil war on the island. The announcement said that Makarios was dead and the National Guard was in complete control of the situation, except for a few pockets of resistance. By the afternoon Nicos Sampson, the notorious EOKA killer, was installed as 'President' in Makarios's place.

But Makarios was not dead. He had had another lucky escape. The Turkish Cypriot Bayrak Radio announced at 15.20 hrs on the day of the coup that Archbishop Makarios had managed to leave the presidential palace and had taken refuge in a mountain hideout in the Paphos area where violent clashes were taking place. The news broadcast by Bayrak Radio was later confirmed by a broadcast from Makarios himself from his hideout. He urged his supporters to fight and resist the Junta's coup.

A few days later Makarios told his own story to the UN Security Council in New York (see Appendix 4). He said that on the second day of the coup he had decided to leave Cyprus to avoid falling into the hands of the Junta. He was airlifted from the Paphos bishopric, where he had taken refuge, to the British Bases and from there was flown to Malta and thence to London.

Makarios told the Security Council that the Greek military regime had openly violated the independence of Cyprus and had extended its dictatorship to the island. He claimed that the coup was a flagrant violation of the independence and sovereignty of the Republic of Cyprus. About the situation in the island, he said, 'I am afraid that the number of casualties is large and that the material destruction is heavy . . . our primary concern at present is the ending of the tragedy'. He pointed out that the events in Cyprus were not an internal affair for the Greek Cypriots alone, but that the Turkish Cypriots were also affected. Both Greeks and Turks would suffer from the consequences of the Junta's invasion.

During the days that followed the coup the situation in Cyprus was indeed tragic. More than 5,000 Makarios supporters were put behind bars and the rival Greek Cypriot armed groups were mercilessly slaughtering each other. Foreign news reports from Cyprus confirmed Archbishop Makarios's statement to the Security Council that the losses were heavy and that both Greeks and Turks were suffering. A report in the *Washington Star News* on 22 July 1974 said:

> Bodies littered the streets and there were mass burials . . . People who were told by Makarios to lay down their guns were shot out of hand by the National Guard. They were buried in mass graves . . . There were 14 Turkish Cypriots who fled to the safety of a school and barricaded themselves in. They were surrounded by the National Guard and when they surrendered they were all killed.

On 23 July 1974, *The Times* of London quoted the American wife of Dr Lyssarides (head of the EDEK Party, Democratic Union of the Centre) saying that many supporters of Makarios had been massacred during and after the coup. Mrs Lyssarides claimed that she had been told by sources she trusted that about 100 members of the presidential guard were killed after they had laid down their arms. On 25 July 1974 *Combat*, published in Belgium, reported: 'It has been confirmed that during the days following the coup in Nicosia at least 2,000 of Makarios's supporters have either been killed in the fighting or executed.'[29]

While the Greek Cypriots were locked in a deadly internecine war the Turkish Cypriots, surrounded by hostile forces and caught in the crossfire between pro- and anti-Makarios elements, were in mortal peril. If Nicos Sampson, a staunch enemy of the Turks, and his master in Athens were to win the day the Turkish Cypriots knew the fate which awaited them. 'Orders of the day' were later discovered in Greek military camps showing that Greece had made detailed preparations for a takeover of Cyprus. At the time it also seemed as if the USA was about to recognise the Nicos Sampson government and the Turks were afraid that Great Britain might do likewise. Therefore Turkey had to act quickly.

22 *The Turkish Intervention*

Turkey, as one of the guarantors of the Cyprus Republic, could not accept the Greek *fait accompli* against the independence and sovereignty of the republic, nor could it stand by and watch Turkish Cypriots being killed or put under the Greek colonial yoke. The Prime Minister of Turkey, Bulent Ecevit, flew to London on 17 July 1974 to try to convince the British government that, as the two guarantors, they should jointly intervene to prevent a complete takeover of Cyprus by Greece. Great Britain, however, would not act. Turkey was left with no alternative but to move alone under Article 4 (2) of the Treaty of Guarantee to protect the independence of the island and to put an end to the terrible destruction of life and property. So, on 20 July 1974, Turkey sent a peace force which landed in northern Cyprus.

The Turkish Premier issued a statement announcing that the Turkish armed forces were engaged in a peace operation in Cyprus to end decades of strife provoked by extremist and irredentist elements. These elements were now killing their own people, the Greek Cypriots. He said that Turkey's action was not an invasion but an act against invasion. He declared that the Turkish peace force would not open fire unless fired upon and that Turkish planes were not dropping bombs but messages of goodwill to the peoples of Cyprus.[30] Indeed, thousands of leaflets in both Greek and Turkish were dropped by Turkish planes at the start of the operation which briefly explained Turkey's peaceful aims. Security passes were also dropped over Greek areas to ensure the safe conduct of anyone who wished to move from the operation zone into safer areas.

The Turkish Cypriot Bayrak Radio repeated at frequent intervals a message from the Turkish Vice-President of the republic, declaring that the intervention was not directed against the Greek community with whom the Turks of Cyprus wished to live on friendly terms as co-founders of independence. The object of the operation was to eliminate the pro-Junta elements who had, by the use of force, usurped the rights and freedom of the Greek Cypriot community.

However, all Turkish appeals and warnings were disregarded for Nicos Sampson, who with a Greek army officer had planned the complete extermination of the Turkish community during the 1963–4 period,[31] realised that he could turn the intervention to his own advantage. The arrival of the common enemy would unite all Greek Cypriots, and accordingly he opened the prison doors and let out the Makarios supporters he had imprisoned. He also gave them guns to fight the Turks. The Greek Cypriot radio began issuing false news bulletins about the Turks being driven into the sea in panic.

The Greek Cypriot National Guard facing the Turkish peace force was not an ill-equipped, badly trained militia. It was equipped with all kinds of modern weapons and possessed large stocks of ammunition. The Greek High Command and the Greek Cypriot administration had, during the previous eleven years, constructed extensive fortifications along the northern face of the Kyrenia range of mountains. From these positions Turkish officers and soldiers were being shot and killed on the shores of the island they had come to save from anarchy, bloodshed and colonisation.

The Turkish Cypriot community was also enduring a new and terrible ordeal. All Turkish villages and towns were being attacked throughout the island by mobile units of the

69

National Guard. The pattern of the onslaught resembled that of 1963, the only difference this time being that the attacks were more vicious and more destructive than before. The Turkish Cypriot defenders put up a stiff resistance but they had little success because of the superior numbers and arms of their adversaries. Within a few days almost all Turkish enclaves, except for the main Nicosia enclave, were occupied by the Greeks. Twenty-one thousand more Turkish Cypriots were driven out of twenty-seven villages; 35,880 were held as hostages in eighty villages; and 26,150 were surrounded in sixty villages. In the towns of Limassol, Paphos and Larnaca, all Turkish males between the ages of 14 and 60 were separated from their families and held as hostages in open football stadiums. Thus while the men baked under the July sun, their defenceless children and women-folk shivered with fear in their lonely homes not knowing what indignity or torture awaited them. This sadistic behaviour on the part of the Greek and Greek Cypriot armed elements eventually led to the frantic rush of Turkish Cypriots to the safety of the Turkish-controlled north.

The following is an excerpt from a report sent by Terence Smith from Limassol at the time and published in the *Herald Tribune* on 25 July 1974:

On the sun-baked dirt floor of the Municipal Soccer Stadium here, about 1,750 men from Limassol's Turkish enclave and the surrounding Turkish villages are penned behind cells of barbed wire.

Their days are spent sheltering under the scorching sun that sends temperatures into high 90s, their nights shivering in the damp breezes that blow from the sea. Greek Cypriot National Guardsmen keep watch on them from machinegun positions in the upper seats of the stadium.

Although the men are dressed in street clothes and claim

to be civilians, they are being held as prisoners of war by the Greek Cypriots.

Conditions in Larnaca were no better. Eight hundred and seventy-three males between 12 and 90 had been herded into a building which could scarcely accommodate 100 people. A prominent member of the Turkish community of Larnaca, Mr Alper Faik Genç, who was a prisoner himself, describes the conditions of the Larnaca camp as follows:

We suffered from sleeplessness and stress. We had nothing to eat except five olives a day and a piece of bread. A thin slice of cheese was added to our daily ration and a tin of sardines was shared by six prisoners every other day. A certain Greek Cypriot woman called ELSI HARALAMBIDES who resided opposite the camp – being a member of EOKA B's women's wing – was responsible for inciting Greek fanatics to stop delivery of bread to the prisoners and for urging Greek groups to ill-treat the Turks. There was no doctor. No medicine. Two of our people died as a result of 'twisted intestines'; or that was the explanation given by the Greeks, who did not care to have an autopsy of the dead.[32]

About the third day of the Turkish intervention an unexpected change took place on the Greek side. Nicos Sampson handed over the 'presidency' to Glafcos Clerides who accepted the office, as he explained, in order to help Cyprus. Mr Clerides took the oath of office in the presence of a defrocked dissident bishop and made his first appeal to Greek Cypriots as the 'President of Cyprus'. He led the government with the ministers of the coup for five months.

The foreign ministers of Turkey, Greece and Great Britain held talks in Geneva from 25 to 30 July 1974, and on the last day of their meeting they signed a joint peace declaration on Cyprus. After the signing of the declaration, the British Foreign Secretary, Mr Callaghan, was reported to have said: 'It creates conditions under which Greece and Turkey can draw back honourably from making war on each other.'[33]

The Geneva Declaration specifically provided that: (3) . . .

B. All the Turkish enclaves occupied by Greek or Greek Cypriot forces should be immediately evacuated. These enclaves will continue to be protected by UNFICYP and to have their previous security arrangements. Other Turkish enclaves outside the area controlled by the Turkish Armed Forces shall continue to be protected by an UNFICYP security zone and may as before maintain their own police and security forces . . .
D. Military personnel and civilians detained as a result of the recent hostilities shall either be exchanged or released under the supervision of the International Committee of the Red Cross within the shortest possible time.

The three foreign ministers also noted, significantly, 'the existence in practice in the Republic of Cyprus of two autonomous administrations, that of the Greek Cypriot community and that of the Turkish Cypriot community'.

When the three foreign ministers and representatives of the Greek and Turkish Cypriot communities met in Geneva for further discussions on 8 August 1974, as decided at the first Geneva meeting, it was found that none of the agreed provisions of the Geneva Declaration had been implemented by the Greek side. The Turkish enclaves were still under Greek occupation, thousands of Turkish Cypriots were still being held as hostages, and armed Greek elements were still harassing Turkish Cypriots and committing brutal atrocities. The Greek side resorted to deception and delaying tactics. They obstructed any discussion of the basic issues, claiming that these were not within the competence of the conference, and insisted on the withdrawal of the Turkish forces from Cyprus. When, finally, the Turkish Foreign Minister tabled a conciliatory proposal for 'cantonal federation' as a basis for solution, the Greek Cypriot representative rejected it and demanded a thirty-six-hour recess 'for further consultations in Nicosia'.

The Greek Cypriot representative had gone to Geneva with a large and widely representative team of experts and advisers which obviated the necessity for any consultation in Nicosia. It was obvious that the Greek and Greek Cypriot representatives were trying to gain time in order to regroup their forces in the island and to muster enough international support to lever the Turkish peace force out of Cyprus. The Turkish side possessed information that the Greeks were laying mines around the Turkish areas and bringing new forces from Greece. The Turkish forces occupied an uncomfortably small, triangular region between Kyrenia and Nicosia and the area was vulnerable from both flanks. Turkey's request for a no man's land around the Turkish forces was rejected. The time factor was vitally important and therefore Turkey insisted on an agreement at least in principle. Moreover, the Greek side was not willing to compromise. News of genocide in the Messaoria electrified the whole situation and so, on 14 August 1974, the second Turkish operation began.

Explaining the reasons which necessitated the second operation, the Turkish Premier said:

Having reached the conclusion that there is no use but only harm in maintaining the appearance of continuing a conference that is being internationally obstructed and the deliberations of which are unilaterally violated, Turkey has considered it her duty to fulfil by herself her prerogatives and duties as a guarantor power, and her responsibilities concerning the independence of Cyprus as well as the rights and security of the Turkish Cypriot people.

The action now undertaken by Turkey is at least as rightful and legal as the action she started on July 20, as a guarantor power and strictly within the bounds of her authority as such a power, for the same conditions exist today as on the 20th July – conditions that formed the basis of the rightfulness and legality of her action. This new Turkish action is as legitimate as Turkey's initial move and is its logical conclusion.[34]

After a three-day action, freeing Turkish areas and preventing massacres, the Turkish forces stopped their operation on 16 August 1974.

Following the ceasefire on 16 August 1974, Turkey invited Greece and the Greek Cypriots to a new conference between the three guarantor powers and the representatives of the Greek and Turkish communities for a discussion on a final settlement of the Cyprus problem. Premier Ecevit reiterated that Turkey would be understanding and flexible on the revision of the demarcation line and would speed up the phased reduction of her forces. However, Greece and the Greek Cypriots rejected the offer.

The trail of blood and mass graves discovered after the second operation horrified not only the Turks but also the international mass media. Virtually the entire population of three Turkish villages (Aloa, Sandallaris and Maratha), including young babies and men and women in their 80s, had been massacred and dumped in mass graves. Eight-four male Turkish Cypriots, between 13 and 74 years of age, had been taken away from the villages of Tokhni, Mari and Zyyi and machine-gunned outside Pallodia in the Limassol District. The German newspaper *Die Zeit* wrote on 30 July: 'The massacres of Turks in Paphos and Famagusta are the proof of how justified the Turks were to undertake their second intervention.'

Perhaps the most significant confirmation justifying Turkey's intervention came from Nicos Sampson himself. In an interview with the Athens newspaper *Apoyevmatini* on 15 July 1975, the first anniversary of the coup, he disclosed that he was 'about to declare Enosis' when he was forced to quit the presidency. This illustrates the gravity of the threat to the independence of Cyprus immediately after the coup and the danger of a full-scale war between Turkey and Greece.

Regarding the outcome of the second Geneva meeting, the Minority Rights Group Report no. 30 of 1976, p. 4, stated:

> Although not participating directly in the talks, the uncompromising spirit of Makarios weighed heavily over the Greek Cypriot delegation. Greece itself was in the throes of political convulsions following the removal of the Junta. There was little coordination, little awareness of Turkey's determination and the unfortunate overconfidence that somehow, unbelievably, the status quo could be restored, mainly with pressure from Britain and the United States.

After the second operation important developments occurred in quick succession. The UN Secretary-General visited the island between 25–26 August 1974 and had consultations with the Greek and Turkish Cypriot sides which resulted in the commencement of bilateral talks in Nicosia between myself and Mr Glafcos Clerides. These talks were conducted weekly in the presence of the UN Secretary-General's Special Representative in Cyprus and dealt with humanitarian issues. The release of Turkish and Greek prisoners of war, which began on 23 September 1974 and was completed by the end of October 1974, was a result of these meetings.

23   *Makarios Returns*

During the period immediately after the Turkish peace operation, Makarios concentrated on disseminating anti-Turkish propaganda abroad. The governments of the USA and Great Britain, obviously uncomfortable about Makarios's presence in their countries, urged Turkey to agree to his return to the island. They seemed to believe that if Makarios was to be confronted with the realities in Cyprus, he might cease to be intransigent or even resign. Turkey raised no objection and Makarios returned to Cyprus on 7 December 1974.

Makarios had been away from the island for more than seventy-five days, and according to the constitution he had to submit to a process of re-election. However, ignoring the constitution yet again, he simply took over from Clerides without an election. The Turkish side objected to these illegalities and refused to recognise Makarios as elected President or his regime as the government of Cyprus. Ten days after his arrival, Makarios tried to visit the 10,000 Limassol Turks who had taken refuge in the Paramali British Sovereign Base Area where they were living in a large tented camp under miserable conditions. The Turkish refugees gave him a rough reception.

It soon became clear that Archbishop Makarios had not changed either his attitude or his tactics. During the 1963–74 period he had not been in a hurry to solve the Cyprus problem and he would not change even after all that had happened. He was still satisfied with the results of his own coup in 1963. He had established an exclusively Greek administration in Cyprus and passed it off as the 'government of Cyprus'. As he still held this important tool in his hands, he saw no reason for compromise. He established a National Council as a cover for his intransigence and finally he introduced the 'long struggle' slogan. If the Turks did not agree to his terms, he would lead the Greek Cypriots against the Turks in a new, marathon struggle.

24 *The US Arms Embargo*

During his brief stay in the USA, Archbishop Makarios had carried out extensive propaganda among the Greek-Americans and had incited them to press the US administration to apply sanctions against Turkey. Subsequently the influential 'Greek lobby' in Congress went to work on the Defence Co-operation Agreement between the USA and Turkey which was awaiting ratification by Congress. The ratification of the agreement was postponed and in February 1975 an embargo was imposed on arms supplies to Turkey.

The justification used for the 'embargo' was that Turkey had used NATO arms supplied by the USA during the peace operation in Cyprus. The Greek lobby argued that such use of American arms was contrary to the US Foreign Assistance Act. But the supporters of this argument ignored the fact that the Greek Cypriots had been using US-supplied NATO arms against Turkish Cypriots for over eleven years and that the Greek and Greek Cypriot armed forces in the island were still using them against the Turks.

Turkey called the 'embargo' a grave mistake. She pointed out that the supply of American arms to Turkey was not a favour but an essential obligation under a military defence alliance. The attempt to link the Cyprus issue with the bilateral defence co-operation between Turkey and the USA could only result in the breakdown of co-operation between the two countries. Accordingly, Turkey declared that the new conditions necessitated a rearrangement of her contribution to the defence alliance.[35]

Indeed, the 'embargo' turned out to be a big blunder both in a political and a military sense. During its forty-two month existence, the 'embargo' only accomplished the weakening of the NATO defence system, without bringing the Cyprus problem any nearer to a solution. On the contrary, the 'embargo' became an obstacle to settlement, because it made the Greek leaders in Athens and Nicosia more intransigent than ever before. The 'embargo' was finally lifted on 26 September 1978.

25 *The Vienna Talks*

The bilateral talks on humanitarian issues which had started in August 1974 were suspended after the return of Archbishop Makarios to Cyprus in December 1974, pending clarification of Mr Clerides's authority and terms of reference. These questions were resolved by the first week in January 1975 and the talks were resumed on 14 January 1975. It was agreed to begin the talks with a discussion on the 'powers and functions of the central government in a federal state'.[36]

But once again Makarios started exercising a negative influence by making provocative statements about the futility of the talks and the necessity for getting ready for a 'long struggle'. In view of this obvious insincerity on the Greek side, the autonomous Turkish Cypriot administration was declared the 'Turkish Federated State of Cyprus' on 13 February 1975. The principle of a federal solution had already been accepted and the Turkish Cypriots' action was merely to establish the Turkish wing of the envisaged Federal Republic of Cyprus. In spite of repeated assurances that this was not a 'unilateral declaration of independence', the Greek Cypriots walked out of the talks – not so much to register a protest against the declaration of the Turkish Federated State, as to make an impact on the forthcoming Security Council debate on Cyprus. But the resolution which came out of the Security Council called for the urgent resumption of the intercommunal talks on Cyprus.

After preliminary discussions in Nicosia, it was agreed to

resume the talks in Vienna on 28 April 1975 under the auspices of the UN Secretary-General. The first round of talks lasted up to 3 May and was mainly devoted to 'an exchange of views on the powers and functions of the central government'. A committee was established to facilitate further consideration of the issue. The second round of talks was held on 5 June, and continued for two days during which the central government issue was more extensively discussed. A new proposal, for the establishment of a transitional government, was introduced by the Turkish side.

The third round of talks from 31 July to 2 August was a very important one. During this period the question of the transfer of population was tackled and settled. The Greek side agreed to the transfer of Turks from the south to the north and the Turks agreed to allow Greeks living in Turkish-controlled areas to move to the Greek-controlled south.[37] Until then, the Greek Cypriot leaders had been preventing the movement of Turks to the north and refusing to receive Greeks coming from the north.

The steady progress being made in Vienna was troubling Archbishop Makarios in Nicosia. On the first anniversary of the 15 July coup he delivered a belligerent speech at a mass rally in Nicosia, calling for a 'long struggle for final victory'. After that, the local Greek press began attacking Mr Clerides's handling of the talks and particularly his agreement to the movement of populations. Despite some strict and harsh measures on the part of the Greek Cypriot administration, more than 50,000 Turks had already moved north. In September 10,000 Turkish Cypriots were transferred north with the assistance of UNFICYP. There remained in the south only about 150 Turkish Cypriots, some of them very old people.

The fourth round of talks was held in New York from 8–10 September 1975, but Mr Clerides refused to continue the talks on the grounds that the Turkish side had not submitted concrete proposals on the territorial issue and the meeting was adjourned. It was obvious that Mr Clerides was acting on orders from Nicosia. However, after a delay of five months, the fifth round of talks was held in Vienna on 17 February 1976 as a result of an agreement reached between the Turkish and Greek foreign ministers in Brussels on 12 December 1975.[38] During this round there was extensive discussion on both the territorial and the constitutional issues. It was also agreed that an exchange of written proposals should take place through the UN Secretary-General's Special Representative in Cyprus within six weeks. Mr Clerides agreed to submit the Greek proposals ten days before the Turkish Cypriots to give the Turkish side time to study the Greek proposals and submit, if necessary, counter-proposals. However, when the time came for the submission of proposals Mr Clerides tried to back out of his earlier agreement. He argued that he had agreed to the ten-day arrangement on his personal initiative without consulting the Greek Cypriot leadership in Nicosia. As a result of the ensuing squabble on the Greek side Mr Clerides resigned and Mr Tassos Papadopoullos, a Greek Cypriot deputy, was appointed in his place. This necessitated the appointment of a new interlocutor of equal standing on the Turkish side, but the talks remained in abeyance.

26   *The Denktash–Makarios 'Guidelines'*

To break the ice, I wrote a letter to Archbishop Makarios on 9 January 1977, proposing a direct meeting to discuss all aspects of the Cyprus problem and pointing out that without such a meeting, during which a basic approach to the problem could be worked out, the interlocutors would be unable to make progress even if they were to begin talks. Makarios accepted the invitation and two meetings took place in Nicosia: the first one on 27 January 1977 and the second on 12 February 1977. At the second meeting, which was also attended by theUN Secretary-General, it was agreed to resume the talks in Vienna under the auspices of the UN Secretary-General at the end of March. The following instructions were drawn up as guidelines for the interlocutors as a basis for future negotiations:

1. We are seeking an independent, non-aligned, bi-communal Federal Republic.
2. The territory under the administration of each community should be discussed in the light of economic viability or productivity and land ownership.
3. Questions of principle like freedom of movement, freedom of settlement, the right of property and other specific matters, are open for discussion taking into consideration the fundamental basis of a bi-communal

federal system and certain practical difficulties which may arise for the Turkish Cypriot Community.

4. The powers and functions of the Central Federal Government will be such as to safeguard the unity of the country, having regard to the bi-communal character of the State.[39]

The sixth round of the Vienna talks began on 31 March 1977 and lasted until 7 April 1977. Eleven meetings were held in which both sides put forward detailed views on all issues. However the joint communiqué issued at the end of these talks stated that it had not been possible to bridge the considerable gap between the two sides. The new Turkish Cypriot interlocutor, Mr Ümit Süleyman Onan, told reporters at the end of the talks that the Greek Cypriot proposals on the territorial issue were not consistent with realities. He added, however, that, despite differences of concept and approach on both the territorial and the constitutional aspects, the Turkish side had found the talks very useful. The two sides had had an opportunity to get a better understanding of each other's way of thinking and views.

The Greek Cypriot interlocutor, Mr Tassos Papadopoullos, in contrast, was totally negative. He told reporters that the sixth round of talks had been a complete failure and he blamed this on the Turkish side.

After returning to Nicosia, the interlocutors met on a number of occasions in May and June to overcome their differences and to prepare the ground for the seventh round of talks. But these meetings were held in a somewhat strained atmosphere because the Greek Cypriots had yet again stepped up their anti-Turkish propaganda and were waging an economic war against the Turkish Cypriots. In any case, the projected seventh round of the Vienna talks was torpedoed by the sudden death of Makarios on 3 August 1977.

Throughout his career as a priest-politician, Archbishop

Makarios always maintained that he worked only for the union of Cyprus with Greece. Now, looking back at the battles he waged for this purpose from the day he took the 'Enosis oath' until the day of his death twenty-seven years later, one finds that these struggles have brought nothing but violence, bloodshed and untold human misery to the island and serious threats to the peace of the region. However, the sad irony of it all is that the Greek Cypriots continue to believe that, but for the insane coup of the Greek Junta and Turkey's intervention, Makarios's struggles would have been crowned with final victory. They still look upon Makarios as their 'great' leader. Those who followed him blindly during his lifetime, now promise to follow faithfully his ideals, policies and plans until 'national restoration' is achieved. 'National restoration', needless to say, stands for 'union with Greece'.[40]

27 *Enter Kyprianou*

The death of Archbishop Makarios left a vacuum in the political leadership on the Greek side. The archbishop was an authoritarian who always acted on his own counsel and he had not groomed any one of his close collaborators as his successor. The leader of the Democratic Party, Mr Spyros Kyprianou, who was the President of the Greek Cypriot House of Representatives at the time of the archbishop's death, became Acting President. Seven months later, on 5 February 1978, he was installed, unopposed, as President.

On cogent legal grounds Turkey and the Turkish Cypriot community refused to recognise Kyprianou as the President of the Republic. They regarded him as no more than the leader of the Greek Cypriot community and the head of the Greek Cypriot administration. The Turkish community had serious misgivings about the kind of influence Mr Kyprianou would have on intercommunal relations, for they knew from the statements he used to make as Makarios's Foreign Minister that he, too, was a fanatical exponent of Enosis. The following extracts from only three of Kyprianou's public statements in the period 1963–74 serve to justify the Turkish community's apprehensions:

The national leadership, which voices the wishes of all the people, is not prepared to accept any compromise solution adulterating the people's national restoration. The Cyprus people want union with Greece. The Greek Cypriot people will continue to struggle having as their standard the Greek flag, Greek virtues and Greek ideals. (Greek Cypriot PIO press release no. 13, 16 July 1966)

Cyprus is now an independent and sovereign state and, therefore, the struggle for union with Greece is easier and shorter than before. (Greek Cypriot PIO press release no. 4, 1 April 1967)

The unity of purpose, aim and policy existing between Greece and Cyprus is absolute. The line of policy by the two governments is one and the same. Neither Cyprus nor Greece can possibly accept solutions that might, sooner or later, be considered by the people and history, and by posterity, as nationally inadmissible compromises . . . (Greek Cypriot PIO press release no. 7, 24 March 1971)

Given the strength of his commitment to Enosis it was not surprising that, on becoming President, Kyprianou stated his intention of following in the footsteps of Makarios. When the Turkish side pressed for the resumption of the Vienna talks, Mr Kyprianou adopted an intransigent attitude and demanded new, concrete and substantive proposals. He knew very well that the two sides had already submitted their proposals at the sixth round of talks in Vienna where it had been agreed that the clarifications made, and the points raised then, would be pursued when the talks resumed.[41] In fact, Kyprianou was relying on a Turkish rejection of his demand in order to be able to blame the Turkish side for delaying a settlement.

28 *New Turkish Cypriot Proposals*

In mid-January 1978, the UN Secretary-General visited Cyprus and, at a luncheon he gave in Nicosia, he secured an agreement between myself and Mr Kyprianou on a negotiating procedure for the next round of talks. The agreement was that the Turkish Cypriot side would prepare and submit to the UN Secretary-General proposals on the main aspects of the problem. The UN Secretary-General would then consult with the parties on the best method of resuming the talks. The procedure agreement was widely hailed as a major breakthrough for an early resumption of the talks.

But as soon as the UN Secretary-General had left the island, the Greek Cypriot leadership started a campaign against the talks and the Turkish proposals, on the absurd assumption that they would not be acceptable. This campaign went so far that it even alarmed moderate sections of the Greek Cypriot community. The local Greek weekly newspaper *Alithia* published the following warning on 6 February 1978:

Whenever there are positive developments in the Cyprus issue, dark and extremist forces immediately take action and try to create difficulties and impede progress. The same thing is happening again. Even before the Turkish proposals are submitted, the representatives of a certain political party are touring villages day and night to propagate for the rejection of the proposals and to instigate the people against any agreement.

It is high time we realised that this cannot go on. We are constantly playing with fire. One day we shall have our hands burnt and we shall lose all ability to manoeuvre. The time has come to change tactics. We must put a halt to the people who tour villages to deliver destructive speeches for partisan aims. We must put a categorical halt to the circulation of leaflets full of extremist slogans.

Despite the Greek Cypriot campaign, the Turkish side prepared its proposals and submitted them to the UN Secretary-General in Vienna on 13 April 1978. An explanatory note on the Turkish Cypriot proposals for the solution of the Cyprus problem was also released to the press on the same day (see Appendix 12). After three meetings with the legal and constitutional advisers to the Turkish Cypriot interlocutor, who had personally submitted the proposals, the UN Secretary-General issued a statement on 15 April 1978 in which he said: 'The Turkish Cypriot proposals deal with the constitutional and territorial aspects of the Cyprus problem in a concrete and substantial way.'[42]

The Greek Cypriot leader, Mr Spyros Kyprianou, rejected outright the Turkish Cypriot proposals when they were transmitted to him personally by the UN Secretary-General on 19 April 1978. Mr Kyprianou declared that the 'philosophy and concept' of the Turkish Cypriot proposals were totally unacceptable to his side and, as such, they could not be treated as a basis for the resumption of the talks.

Having fully complied with the procedure agreement reached in Nicosia in January 1978, the Turkish side expected the UN Secretary-General to convene the talks. I had a meeting with the UN Secretary-General at the UN Headquarters in New York on 22 May 1978, after which he issued a statement expressing the Turkish community's support for an immediate resumption of the talks.

In Turkey, Premier Ecevit also expressed the view that the Secretary-General should reconvene the talks. He stressed that the Turkish Cypriot proposals were negotiable in every respect.[43]

Despite the Turkish side's display of goodwill and flexibility, Mr Kyprianou maintained his intransigent attitude and adamantly refused to negotiate.

In his report of 31 May 1978, the UN Secretary-General observed that the cause of a just and peaceful settlement in Cyprus could not be served by calling for talks when there was no agreement on the negotiating basis and when one or other party was not willing to proceed with meaningful negotiations. He also said:

73. . . . There are a number of factors which inevitably come into play in a situation of this kind. In this particular case not only the substance of the proposals submitted but developments elsewhere that were thought likely to affect the Cyprus problem have created a situation in which agreement of both parties to resume the talks has not materialised.[44]

The UN Secretary-General also mentioned that 'one of the parties' had suggested an interest in possible 'alternative approaches'.[45]

From the above observations of the UN Secretary-General, it is easy to identify which side obstructed the resumption of the talks and why. The Turkish side had been urging the resumption of the talks even with an open agenda. The party 'not willing to proceed with meaningful negotiations' and showing interest in 'alternative approaches' was the Greek side. It is also easy to see which 'developments elsewhere' were having a negative effect on the situation, as the struggle

over the fate of the 'embargo' was going on at the time between the US administration and Congress. The Greek side
believed that a resumption of the intercommunal talks would
expedite the lifting of the embargo.

29 *The Issue of Missing Persons*

Having obstructed the UN Secretary-General's efforts to reactivate the intercommunal talks, the Greek side then blocked the setting up of an investigatory body for ascertaining the fate of the missing persons on both sides. Their reason for doing this was that any progress on humanitarian issues would be as fatal for the future of the 'embargo' as progress on political issues.

The question of missing persons is not an issue which affects the Greek Cypriots alone. As mentioned before, the problem of missing persons first arose during the 1963-4 Greek onslaught against the Turkish community when hundreds of Turkish Cypriot civilians were abducted by the so-called Greek Cypriot security forces and never seen again. Hundreds more were to disappear after the Turkish peace operation in 1974.

The problem of the missing persons on the Greek side arose as a result of the 15 July coup during which thousands of Greek Cypriots were killed in the fighting between supporters of the coup and Makarios loyalists. Independent foreign press reports estimated the number of Greek Cypriots killed or executed during the coup at over 2,000. However, the Greek Cypriot authorities have never issued an official casualty list. Despite many eyewitness accounts of mass killings and burials on the Greek side, no serious attempt has been made to trace the culprits and bring them to justice. Even the testimony of a Greek Cypriot priest, Papatsestos (see Appendix 6), who complained to Archbishop Makarios that after the coup he had been forced to bury a wounded young Greek Cypriot along with a heap of dead loyalists and some Turkish Cypriots, was effectively ignored without even a superficial inquiry. The Greek Cypriot authorities blamed the Turks for all their missing persons. They claimed that 2,000 Greek Cypriots had disappeared during the Turkish intervention; curiously enough the exact number reported to have been killed during the coup. Blaming the Turks for their disappearance was a convenient excuse to avoid taking action against the perpetrators and sympathisers of the coup and an excellent pretext for propaganda against Turkey.

The question of missing persons was dealt with, along with other humanitarian issues, at the weekly meetings I had with Mr Clerides, with the assistance of the International Committee of the Red Cross, soon after the ceasefire in August 1974. The ICRC representative stated categorically in the presence of the UN Secretary-General's Special Representative in Cyprus that all prisoners of war taken to Turkey had been returned to the island and delivered to the Greek side. This fact was also confirmed in the report of the head of the ICRC dated 18 March 1977. At the time there were only twenty-three or twenty-four cases pending investigation. The Greek Cypriot officials knew all these facts but they continued to claim that some missing Greek persons were still detained in Turkey.

During the meetings between myself and Archbishop Makarios on 27 January and 12 February 1977, the issue of missing persons was discussed extensively in the presence of the UN Secretary-General (see Appendix 8). Archbishop Makarios pretended that he did not know how many Greek Cypriots were killed during the coup or where they were buried. He admitted that he was using the issue for propaganda purposes and said that this was because he had no other weapon to use against the Turks.[46] The Turkish Cypriot side suggested the setting up of a committee of community representatives, the Red Cross and the Red Crescent with the participation of the ICRC. Two months later this offer was rejected by the Greek Cypriot side (see Papadopoullos's letter, Appendix 7).

In the meantime, however, the Greek Cypriot propaganda machine lost no opportunity in informing the world that Turkey and Turkish Cypriots were hindering the setting up of such a committee.

In 1977 the matter came before the Third Committee of the UN and a unanimous resolution (GAOR, Supplement 45, Res. 128) was adopted on 16 December, the operative paragraphs of which read as follows:

> *Concerned* at the lack of progress towards the tracing and accounting for missing persons in Cyprus;
> *Expressing the hope* that the informal discussions now taking place to establish a joint committee to trace missing persons are successful;
> (1) *Requests* the Secretary-General to provide his good offices through his Special Representative in Cyprus to support the establishment of an investigatory body with the participation of the ICRC which would be in a position to function impartially, effectively and speedily so as to resolve the problem without undue delay;
> (2) *Invites* the parties concerned to continue co-operating in the establishment of the investigatory body and work out the modalities with a view to activating it expeditiously.

Turkey and Turkish Cypriot representatives urged the setting up the committee which the UN resolution envisaged, but the Greek Cypriot side delayed the matter for a further twelve months, a period which was again spent in informing the world that Turkey was refusing to set up the Committee of Investigation. My public statements on this matter are set out in Appendix 8. Nevertheless, when the matter came before the Third Committee in 1978 and the Turkish side put in a draft resolution for the implementation of the previous year's resolution, the Greek Cypriot side submitted amendments and tried to replace ICRC representatives with 'the representative of the Secretary-General'. When this resolution was put to the vote, sixty-seven were in favour, five against and there were fifty abstentions. The Turkish side insisted on the implementation of the 1977 unanimous resolution, for the Turkish Cypriots saw in this move by the Greek Cypriots an attempt to keep this humanitarian problem in the political field as a propaganda stick. At the summit meeting between myself and Mr Kyprianou on 19 May 1979 the Turkish side undertook to get the appropriate authorities to consider a compromise proposal, but the Cabinet was divided on the issue while the Committee of Relatives of Turkish Cypriot Missing Persons insisted on the implementation of the 1977 unanimous resolution (see Appendix 9).

For the record, Turkey and the Turkish Federated State of Cyprus have repeatedly declared in official statements that no Greek or Greek Cypriot was being held as a detainee or a prisoner of war on the Turkish mainland or within the territory under the control of the Turkish Cypriot authorities in north Cyprus. The general view on this issue, which is also shared by foreign observers, is that the great majority of the Greek Cypriot missing persons – whatever their number – must have been killed during the 15 July coup and the rest – who were mostly armed elements – must be presumed to have lost their lives in action during the fighting after the coup.

30 *The Issue of Displaced Persons*

The Greek Cypriot leaders also continue to exploit another humanitarian issue, that of displaced persons, for political propaganda. As in the case of missing persons, they contend that this problem is an entirely new development in the Cyprus conflict which was brought about by the Turkish intervention in the summer of 1974. But the forced movement of population first began in Cyprus with the EOKA attacks on the Turkish Cypriots in 1958, and was followed by the mass flight of nearly one-quarter of the Turkish population of the island into safer areas as a result of the Greek Cypriot onslaught in December 1963. The number of Turkish Cypriot refugees had risen to 65,000 by the end of September 1974, when the Turks in the Greek-controlled south moved north because of the injustice and harsh treatment which they had endured for eleven years from Greek officials, and because of the massacres committed by the Greek armed elements during and after the coup.

The movement of the Greek Cypriots from north to south started after the landing of the Turkish peace force in the island, but this was not due to the use of armed force against them. The exodus was triggered off by the Greek Cypriot radio broadcasts of the time which described the terrible things the Turkish soldiers would do to the Greeks. This scaremongering was intended to make the Greek Cypriots fight more vigorously against the Turkish troops, but instead it created panic among the Greeks who hastily left their homes before the Turkish troops arrived. At a later stage, other Greek Cypriots moved south largely out of fear of possible reprisals from Turkish Cypriots for the atrocities committed against them between 1963 and 1974 and after the peace operation. The Greeks of Varosha, for example, fled because they had learned of the massacre of the entire population of the three Turkish villages of Aloa, Sandallaris and Maratha in Famagusta District.

A report by the Study Mission of the Sub-committee of the Committee of the Judiciary of the United States Senate (October 1974) describes the effect of such 'panic stories' on Greek Cypriots during the first and the second phases of the peace operation as follows:

> Whenever and wherever the Study Mission talked with Greek Cypriot refugees, the story was basically the same: people moved the instant they saw or thought the Turkish army was advancing towards their town or village.

About the second phase of the operation, the report says:

> Greek Cypriots fled the moment there was rumor or sight of military forces – creating a virtual vacuum into which the Turkish army could and did move without resistance and without the presence of people.

The above extracts from the Study Mission's report not only confirm the fact that the Greek Cypriot displaced persons moved out of their areas without any armed force being used against them, but also discredits the wild stories put out by the Greek Cypriot propagandists about the 'brutal treatment of civilians' by the Turkish army.

How could the Turkish troops hurt people who were not

97

there? But no one seems to have been interested in finding out the real reasons for eleven years of terror and oppression, injustice and discrimination which forced 65,000 Turkish Cypriots to abandon their ancestral homes and move north, even risking death at the hands of armed Greek irregulars as they did so.

The Greek side exploited the refugee issue, first by grossly exaggerating the number of Greek Cypriot displaced persons and also by deliberately delaying their rehabilitation.

After the final ceasefire in August 1974, the Greek Cypriot authorities were reported to have declared the number of displaced Greeks to the UN High Commissioner of Refugees as 160,000. This figure included thousands of Greek Cypriots who had moved out of the main towns and villages to hill resorts or to Greek areas during the coup and the peace operation, but who had returned home after the ceasefire. The propaganda figure put out by the Greek Cypriot leaders is around 200,000. However a service note on 'Legal Aspects of the Problem of Refugees in Cyprus', circulated by the Greek Cypriot Attorney-General, Mr Criton Tornarides in 1975, puts the total number of Greek Cypriots who were domiciled in the liberated areas in the north at 128,563. Nevertheless the Greek side has never attempted to show how 200,000 Greeks could be displaced from an area where only 128,563 Greeks were living.

At a mass meeting of Greek Cypriot displaced persons held in Nicosia on 13 October 1975, the general secretary of their committee claimed that 56,300 displaced persons needed permanent accommodation and of these 18,000 were in tented camps. He also claimed that allocation of accommodation to DPs was being delayed to the point of obstruction.[47] But the Greek Cypriot leaders still continue to talk in the UN and on other international platforms of the 200,000 Greek Cypriot displaced persons and of an island dotted with tented refugee camps.

The exaggerated refugee figures bring in lavish aid and the tented camps make good propaganda even when there is no one in them. A UPI report sent out from Nicosia on 24 February 1977, on the occasion of Mr Clark Clifford's visit to Cyprus, reveals how 'conducted tours' of refugee camps by VIPs are stage-managed for maximum effect. Describing Mr Clark Clifford's visit to a Greek refugee camp and the conduct of one of its inmates, the UPI report said:

She and others wailed as Mr. Clifford walked past and climbed into a limousine to leave. Then, her tears drying instantly, she smiled and waved at President Carter's envoy before rejoining the other women on a Government bus that took them home.

Similar shows are invariably put on by the Greek Cypriot authorities when important personalities visit the Greek side.

31 *Aggressive Diplomacy*

The atmosphere of *détente* in intercommunal relations, created by the Denktash–Clerides meetings in January and February 1977, began to wane after Kyprianou's assumption of office and completely vanished when he summarily rejected the Turkish proposals in April 1978.

Kyprianou spent most of May and June 1978 personally campaigning for the continuation of the arms 'embargo' against Turkey. He snubbed everyone – including heads of governments and states – who advocated the lifting of the 'embargo' and counselled the resumption of the intercommunal talks. He called this 'aggressive diplomacy'.[48] Kyprianou used the same 'diplomacy' at home: he castigated his critics as 'disruptive elements' and sacked his negotiator in the talks, Tassos Papadopoullos, for disagreeing with the interpretation of Archbishop Makarios's policy.

Kyprianou's campaign for the 'embargo' proved unproductive for no one wanted it to continue except the Greek Cypriots and Greece. Moreover, Greece wanted the 'embargo' not for the sake of Greek Cypriots but for her own benefit. The Greek Prime Minister, Karamanlis, had been making discreet moves within NATO circles, seeking 'parity' on armaments with Turkey. Catching up with Turkey through increased military aid did not seem feasible; so, levelling Turkey down through the 'embargo' appeared to Greece a quicker way to 'parity' and, given time, to something better. Turkey's loss was Greece's gain. Therefore,

Karamanlis vigorously supported Kyprianou's efforts to keep the 'embargo' going.

On the Cyprus issue, the Greek Premier adopted a rather passive attitude. He declined to take an active part in the efforts to find a solution, claiming that the Cyprus problem was a matter between Cyprus and Turkey. He briefly defined his government's policy on Cyprus as: 'Cyprus decides, Greece supports.' Like Kyprianou, Karamanlis was in no hurry to find a Cyprus settlement. The Greek Cypriot community was not in any physical danger or difficulty; the Greek Cypriot displaced persons had nearly all been settled; and the Greek Cypriot economy was developing by leaps and bounds thanks to the massive financial aid pouring in from the USA, UK and other countries. So, Greece and the Greek Cypriots could afford to wait for full 'national restoration' in Cyprus. But, in any case, Karamanlis's slogan, 'Cyprus decides, Greece supports', is not convincing. On the Greek side, the National Guard is still under the command of Greek generals and officers, and the Greek community continues to regard Athens as the 'national capital' where all military and political decisions are taken. Kyprianou does not make any move without first consulting the Greek Government.

It is relevant to mention here that Karamanlis ostensibly adopted a somewhat similar attitude after the establishment of the Cyprus Republic in 1960. But it has since been revealed that the Akritas Plan envisaging Enosis (see Appendix 11) was drawn up by senior Greek army officers and that Makarios's underground army was equipped with large quantities of rifles, machineguns, grenades, revolvers and bazookas sent by Greece between 1962 and 1963.[49]

When the US arms embargo was finally lifted in September 1978, Greece and the Greek Cypriot leaders switched their attention to the UN as an instrument for bringing pressure to bear on Turkey. Kyprianou unleashed his 'aggressive diplomacy' in the UN and other international conferences by complaining about Turkey's failure to comply with the UN resolutions on Cyprus and declaring that he would seek a solution only through the UN. He then persuaded the Greek Cypriot political parties that the wisest policy was to turn to the UN General Assembly, to secure a 'tough' resolution and to get it implemented by the Security Council through sanctions.

32 *Greek Cypriots Seek a 'Cheque' from the UN*

The Greek Cypriot political parties are divided by ideological differences, but they forget all their differences and co-operate in the face of the common enemy, the Turks, and pursue a common goal, Enosis. Even the Greek Cypriot Communist Party (AKEL) is committed to the Enosis policy by a standing resolution of its party congress.[50] Therefore, it was not difficult for Kyprianou to secure the co-operation of the party leaders to seek UN help against the Turkish side. An all-party delegation, composed of party leaders, was dispatched to New York for lobbying in and outside the UN and public demonstrations were organised in Nicosia to impress foreign missions. The whole exercise was regarded as a commercial transaction by the Greek Cypriot leaders. They talked about securing a 'cheque' from the General Assembly and then getting it 'cashed' by the Security Council.

The UN General Assembly debated the Cyprus issue early in November 1978, in the absence of Turkish Cypriot representation. Because of certain procedural rules of convenience, the Turkish community is only allowed a cursory hearing in the Special Political Committee and denied a voice in the plenary session where the actual debate takes place. This arrangement, which is unfair to the Turks, is particularly advantageous to the Greek side because it can speak both for the Greek community and also for the so-called Cyprus government and even vote for its own case.[51]

The Turkish Permanent Representative in the UN, addressing the Assembly on behalf of both Turkey and the Turkish Cypriot community, pointed out that the Greek Cypriot leadership, which enjoyed many advantages 'under the feathers of the government of Cyprus', could see no reason to negotiate for a solution which would mean the sharing of the power now absolutely in their hands. He emphasised the importance of the intercommunal talks and reiterated that Turkey had no territorial aspirations in Cyprus. Turkey's intervention in Cyprus had taken place because of the necessity of preventing the annihilation of the Turkish community and safeguarding the independence of the island. He urged the Assembly not to adopt a resolution that would discourage the resumption of the intercommunal talks under the auspices of the UN Secretary-General. Similar appeals were made by other delegates but the Assembly adopted a resolution which, in the words of the US delegate, 'would not promote an atmosphere conducive to the resumption of negotiations'.[52]

One of the negative elements in the resolution which appeared most likely to impede the resumption of the talks was the paragraph which recommended that the 'Security Council examines the question of the implementation, within a time-frame, of its relevant resolutions and considers and adopts, if necessary, all appropriate and practical measures under the Charter for implementation of the UN resolution on Cyprus'. The US delegate had pointed out during the debate that this recommendation was 'unacceptable' because it was misleading to suggest that Security Council action was called for.

A separate vote taken on the offending paragraph brought the majority vote registered on the whole of the resolution from 110 down to 80, and raised the number of abstentions from 22 to 48.

Turkey characterised the resolution as one-sided and deplored the failure of the UN General Assembly to take note of the important developments, such as the 'guidelines' agreed between myself and the late Archbishop Makarios. The Turkish Cypriot side also described the resolution as one-sided and declared that it would not be bound by a resolution taken in its absence. However, I announced my readiness to resume the talks immediately, if the Greek Cypriot side would now come to the negotiating table.

Although the General Assembly resolution called for the urgent resumption of the talks between the two communities on an equal footing, the Greek Cypriot side was in no mood for negotiation. It applied immediately for a Security Council meeting, so as to cash the 'cheque' it had just received from the General Assembly.

The Security Council met and debated the Greek Cypriot application but it did not consider any measure under the Charter for which the Greeks were pressing. The Security Council called upon the parties concerned to comply and co-operate in the implementation of the UN resolutions within a specific time-frame – without specifying any time limit. It urged the representatives of the two communities to resume negotiations under the auspices of the UN Secretary-General and asked him to report on the negotiations and on the progress towards the implementation of its resolutions by 30 May 1979, or earlier, should developments warrant it.

The Security Council discussion on Cyprus was more to the point than the General Assembly debate. This was because of the Council's readiness to hear both sides of the Cyprus question. The Turkish Cypriot side was there to put its case and to challenge allegations made by the other side. In a lengthy address, I analysed the causes of the intercommunal conflict and its consequences and related in detail the terrible experiences of the Turkish community

beginning with the EOKA terror campaign in 1955 right up
to the summer of 1974 (see Appendix 10).

Conclusion

The intercommunal talks on the Cyprus problem have re-started after an interval of two years. The fact that these talks have been going on since 1968, with interruptions, does not encourage one to expect an imminent settlement. The UN Secretary-General, Kurt Waldheim, has publicly endorsed the Turkish position, which is based on the Makarios–Denktash guidelines and envisages a bi-zonal federal system with due regard to Turkish Cypriot security, and has thus exposed the frivolous nature of the artificial delay in talks caused by the Greek Cypriots. However, the Greek Cypriots are maintaining their total economic embargo and propaganda attacks against a quarter of the island's population, namely the Turkish Cypriots, and the removal of this inhuman embargo will be one of the most important questions on the agenda of the talks. Since 1974 Turkish Cypriots have not been subjected to the kind of Greek armed attacks and harassment which they suffered between 1963 and 1974 and this situation allows the holding of talks on the basis of equality. A number of foreign diplomats have recently reported signs of great flexibility on the Greek Cypriot side and one can only hope that events will justify their optimism.

However, the Greek Orthodox Church, which has created the Cyprus problem through its pursuit of Enosis, is still heavily involved in Greek Cypriot politics. Thus any Greek Cypriot politician aspiring to lead his community has to accept the dictates of the church. The Cypriot church continues to dream of ultimate union between Greece and

Cyprus in spite of all that has happened. Unfortunately, young Greek Cypriots are still taught to believe that Enosis is a credible possibility and that support for the idea is their 'national duty'. Underground organisations, successors to EOKA, continue to infest south Cyprus.

In the meantime, Turkey and Greece are trying to settle their various bi-lateral differences. Cyprus continues to be the fulcrum on which the Turkey–Cyprus–Greece triangle is delicately balanced.

Notes

1 H. D. Purcell. *Cyprus* (London: Ernest Benn, 1969), p. 204.

2 On 8 November 1966, Archbishop Makarios (speaking for the union of Crete with Greece – Enosis – at Arkadi Monastery in Crete during the centenary celebrations of the insurrection, and murder, of the Moslem Turkish population of that island) stated: 'Cyprus is here today in this holy place . . . to reiterate once again that she will continue with determination and perseverance her struggle for union with Greece. We shall not abandon our ramparts until the final victory, the realisation of Enosis . . . Cyprus always draws her inspiration from the struggles and sacrifices of Crete. The eternal desire of Cyprus is to unite with motherland Greece and fight for Greece. Our only and invariable aim is Enosis . . . The desire and aspiration of the Greek Cypriots is to unite Cyprus as a whole with the national body. We took over Cyprus as an undivided Greek island. We have preserved it as such. Now, we shall deliver it undivided to the mother's bosom.'

3 Makarios assumed command of the Enosis campaign in 1950 against the background of a long Greek nationalist tradition, a tradition with an organisational and ideological side to it. See Zenon Stavrinides, *The Cyprus Conflict* (Nicosia, 1975).

4 The 'oath' was taken by Makarios, Grivas and ten others, including a Greek general, Nicolas Papadopoullos. See *Memoirs of General Grivas* (London: Longman, 1964), p. 20.

5 In a speech at the village of Panayia on 4 September 1963 Archbishop Makarios declared: 'Unless this small Turkish community forming a part of the Turkish race which has been the terrible enemy of Hellenism is expelled, the duty of the heroes of EOKA can never be considered as terminated.'

6 'The reader may take it that, having signed the London Agreement, Makarios had no intention of allowing the resultant Constitution to stand.' Purcell, op. cit., p. 306.

7 Purcell says that 'by December there were 5,000 fully-trained Greek irregulars and a further 5,000 partially trained' (op. cit., p. 319).

8 Purcell points out that 'Greek Embassy families were being sent home' (op. cit., p. 323).

9 *The Times*, 1 January 1964.

10 Reported in almost all Greek Cypriot newspapers on 28 October 1964.

11 In his report, the mediator expressed a personal conviction that 'the treaties and the constitution were the main cause of the Cyprus dispute.' This was the propaganda line used by the Greek Cypriots. However, the former President of the Supreme Constitutional Court of Cyprus, Prof. Ernst Forsthoff, had described the cause of the conflict in the following terms to a UPI correspondent on 30 December 1963: 'All this has happened because Makarios wanted to remove all constitutional rights from

Turkish Cypriots. From the moment Makarios started openly to deprive Turkish Cypriots of their rights, the present events were inevitable.'

12 Greek Cypriot leaders refused to take back Turkish Cypriot civil servants or pay their salaries and other dues on the ground that all these matters would be part of a political settlement. See the UN Secretary-General's report no. S/5950, 10 September 1964, para. 108.

13 Z. M. Nedjatigil, 'Cyprus Constitutional Proposals and Developments' (PIO, Turkish Federated State of Cyprus, 1977), p. 20.

14 See Appendix 1 for map showing Turkish areas where resistance to the unconstitutional Greek rule continued.

15 The grant provided for under the constitution is £400,000.

16 Archbishop Makarios in a letter dated 9 March 1972, addressed to the three senior bishops of the Cyprus Synod.

17 *Cyprus*, Minority Rights Group Report no. 30 (London, 1976), p. 8. MRG is an international research and information unit registered in Britain as an educational trust under the Charities Act of 1960.

18 Purcell, op. cit., p. 326.

19 On 27 June 1979, the *Guardian* wrote that the continued use by the Greek Cypriots, under the cover of being a government, of all international aid and credit was a valid reason for the Greek Cypriot side not to settle the Cyprus problem.

20 The Kophinou operation was mounted despite the warnings of the UN Secretary-General's Special Representative in Cyprus. A comprehensive account of the operation is given in the UN Secretary-General's special report no. S/8248 and add. 1–9.

21 On 2 February 1966, on the occasion of the visit of Archbishop Makarios to Athens, a joint communiqué was issued to the effect that the two governments objected to any solution ruling out the island's union with Greece.

22 Makarios's declaration was repeated the same day in the evening news bulletin of the Cyprus Broadcasting Station.

23 UN Secretary-General's report no. S/10401, 30 November 1971, para. 79.

24 UN Secretary-General's report no. S/10664, 26 May 1972, paras 30 and 58.

25 Mr Clerides's statement was made in a speech at Omorphita and was reported in the *Cyprus Mail*, 8 August 1976.

26 Manifesto issued by the National Front and published in the local Greek newspaper *Alithia*, 28 June 1969.

27 UN Secretary-General's report no. S/10199, 20 May 1971.

28 Makarios's public statement on the 'internal situation in Cyprus', 29 October 1971.

29 Further quotations from international press reports are given in Appendix 2.

30 Official statement issued by Premier Ecevit on 20 July 1973, explaining the purpose of Turkey's intervention.

31 The plan was mentioned by Archbishop Makarios in an interview with the Italian journalist, Oriana Fallaci, in New York. Makarios told Fallaci that Nicos Sampson and Brig. Ioannides (who was serving in Cyprus during the 1963–4 period and who was to emerge later as the strongman of the Greek Junta in the period before the July coup) visited him one day and suggested that they should attack the Turkish Cypriots suddenly and eliminate them to the last man. The interview was published in the *Washington Post*, 17 November 1974.

32 Alper Faik Genç, *Cyprus Report: From My 1974 Diary* (Nicosia, October 1978), pp. 110–11.

33 *The Times* (31 July 1974).

34 Quote from the Turkish Prime Minister, Mr Ecevit's statement on 14 August 1974 (*Hurriyet* and *Milliyet* and Turkish Cypriot Press, 15 August 1974).

35 Statement by the Turkish Premier, Prof. Sadi Irmak, published in the Turkish press on 6 February 1975.

36 Joint statement issued by Denktash and Clerides on 8 January 1975.

37 Joint communiqué issued in Vienna on 2 August 1975.

38 The text of the Brussels agreement was released to the press by the Turkish and Greek foreign ministries on 22 May 1976.

39 UN Secretary-General's report no. S/12323, 30 April 1977, para. 4. See also Appendix 5.

40 In a message to the Greek Cypriot people on the 150th anniversary of Greek Independence, Archbishop Makarios said: 'National restoration has not yet been completed. But Cyprus has faith and follows others' examples. With a solid, internal front, with domestic concord and unity, as dictated by certain lessons of the 1821 struggle, Cyprus will always remain faithful to Greece, its motherland, goal of its struggles and target of the sacrifices of its sons.'

41 UN Secretary-General's report no. S12323, 30 April 1977.

42 UN Secretary-General's report no. S/12723, 31 May 1978, para. 52.

43 ibid., paras 55 and 58.

44 ibid., para. 73.

45 ibid., para. 76.

46 Minutes of the discussion on 'missing persons' were released to the press on 27 October 1977, because of continued false propaganda by the Greek side. The full text of the minutes is given in Appendix 8.

47 The news of the mass meeting and the figures given out by the general secretary of DPs were published in the local Greek newspapers *Agon*, *Phileleftheros* and *Haravghi* on 14 October 1975.

48 Public statement by Mr Kyprianou on 17 June 1978.

49 Disclosure by Mr Glafcos Clerides in the House of Representatives on 31 January 1967. The local Greek daily newspaper *Mahi* published a similar disclosure on 2 February 1967.

50 This resolution was adopted at AKEL's 11th Congress held in Nicosia in 1966, and has not been revoked.

51 The Assembly of the Council of Europe does not allow a purely Greek Cypriot delegation to represent Cyprus and demands the inclusion of Turkish Cypriot members in the Cyprus delegation. Because of this condition the Greek Cypriots boycott Assembly meetings.

52 UN Document, A/33/PV.49, 9 November 1978, p. 51.

Appendices

Appendix 1 :   *Maps Showing Turkish*
                 Communities Attacked by
                 Greeks in the 1955–8 EOKA
                 Campaign for Enosis and
                 the Location of Completely
                 Destroyed Turkish Villages
                 and Houses

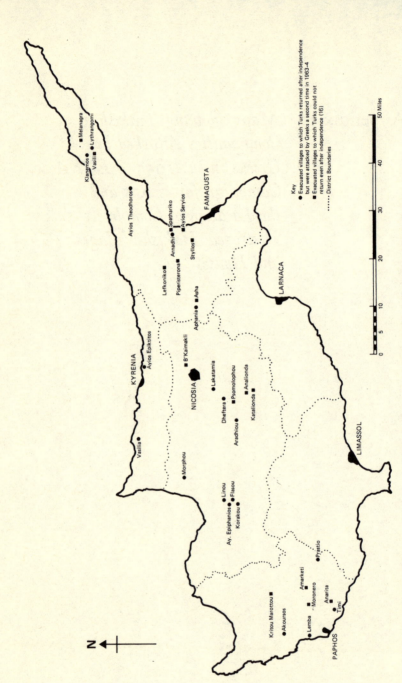

Map 1 *Turkish Communities Attacked by Greeks in the 1955–8 EOKA Campaign for Enosis*

Key

● Evacuated villages to which Turks returned after independence but were attacked by Greeks a second time in 1963–4

■ Evacuated villages to which Turks could not return even after independence (16)

···· District Boundaries

0 5 10   20   30   40   50 Miles

N

KYRENIA
NICOSIA
FAMAGUSTA
LARNACA
LIMASSOL
PAPHOS

Klangnos ■ Melenaga
Vasili ■ Lythrangomi
Avios Theodharos ●
Spathariko
Arnadhi ■ ■ Avios Servios
Lefkoniko ■ Styllos ■
Piperisterona ■
Aphania ● ▲ Asha
Avios Epiktitos ●
Vasilia ●
Morphou ●
B'Kaimakli ■
Lakatamia ●
Dhettera ● Psomolophou ■
Aradhiou ● Analionda ■
Katalionda ●
Av. Epiphanios ● Linou ●
Korakou ● Flasou ●
Prastio ●
Amarketi ■
Kritou Marottou ■ Moronero
Akouros ● Anarita ●
Lemba ■ Timi

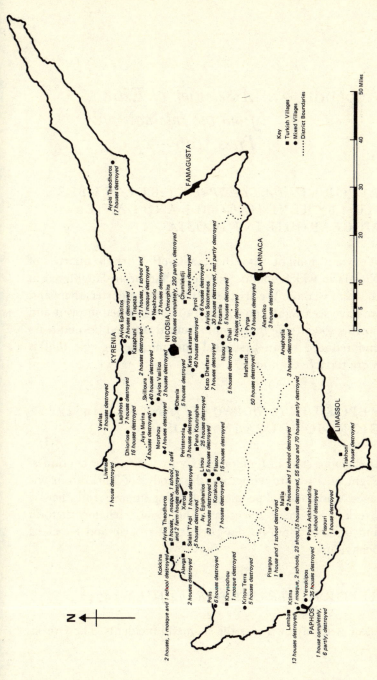

Map 2   *Location of Completely Destroyed Turkish Villages and Houses*

Appendix 2: *A Selection of Extracts from the International Press, 1963–74*

REPORT IN *DAILY EXPRESS* (28 DECEMBER 1963) BY RENE MACCOLL AND DANIEL MCCEARCHIE IN NICOSIA

We went tonight into the sealed-off Turkish quarter of Nicosia in which 200 to 300 people had been slaughtered in the last five days. We are the first Western reporters there and we have seen sights too frightful to be described in print and horrors so extreme that people seemed stunned beyond tears and reduced to an hysterical and mirthless giggle that is more terrible than tears.

REPORT IN *IL GIORNO* (14 JANUARY 1964) BY GIORGIO BOCCA IN NICOSIA

Discussions start in London; in Cyprus, the terror continues. Right now we are witnessing the exodus of Turks from villages. Thousands of people abandoning homes, lands, herds: Greek terrorism is relentless. This time, Hellenic rhetoric and busts of Plato do not cover up barbaric and ferocious behaviour.

REPORT IN *FRANCE SOIR* (24 JULY 1974)

I saw with my own eyes the shameful incidents. The Greeks

burned down Turkish mosques and set fire to Turkish homes in the villages around Famagusta. Defenceless Turkish villagers, who have no weapons, live in an atmosphere of terror created by Greek marauders, and they evacuate their homes and go and live in tents in the forests. The Greeks with their bazookas create total chaos in the Turkish villages. The Greeks' actions bring shame to humanity. Those Turks who can save their lives run to the nearby hills and are able to do nothing but watch the callous looting of their homes.

EXTRACTS FROM A REPORT IN *DAILY TELEGRAPH* (14 JANUARY 1964):

Graves of 12 Shot Turks Found in Cyprus Village

Silent crowds gathered tonight outside the Red Crescent hospital in the Turkish sector of Nicosia, as the bodies of 9 Turks found crudely buried outside the village of Ayios Vassilios, 13 miles away, were brought to the hospital under an escort of the Parachute Regiment. Three more bodies, including one of a woman, were discovered nearby but they could not be moved.

Turks guarded by paratroops are still trying to locate the bodies of 20 more believed to have been buried on the same site. All are believed to have been killed during fighting around the village at Christmas.

Family of Seven

It is thought that a family of seven Turks who disappeared from the village may be buried there. Their house was found burnt, and grenades had been dropped through the roof.

Shallow graves had apparently been hurriedly scooped by

a bulldozer. The bodies appeared to have been piled in two or three deep. All had been shot.

One man had his arms still tied behind his legs in a crouching position and had been shot through the head. A stomach injury indicated that a grenade may have been thrown into his lap.

EXTRACT FROM A REPORT IN THE *GUARDIAN* (20 FEBRURAY 1964)

Day by day and as murder follows murder detached observers here find it harder and harder to credit the Government of Cyprus with any real determination to stamp out violence. If the President really wants peace on earth and to restore the rule of law he could start by investigating publicly the circumstances surrounding last Thursday's attack on the Turkish inhabitants of Limassol. The known facts are that on Wednesday the British peace keeping forces were assured by the Greek authorities that no attack would be made on the Turkish Community. Accordingly the British Army did not patrol the town. At 5.30 the following morning Greek Cypriot security forces launched what our special correspondent describes as 'a heavy well organised attack against the Turkish quarter of Limassol'. It was carried out by hundreds of steel helmeted men armed with automatic weapons and supported by one tank and two armoured bulldozers. If the Greek Cypriot authorities connived at this formidable attack their behaviour is inexcusable. If they were ignorant of its coming they must forfeit their claim to govern and control their own people, let alone the whole Cypriot Community.

EXTRACT FROM A REPORT IN *LE FIGARO* (25–6 JANUARY 1964) BY MAX CLOS

... I have seen in a bathtub the bodies of a mother and of

her three young children murdered just because their father was a Turkish officer . . .

Archbishop Makarios is too much of an ecclesiastic to express himself so brutally, but it is a fact that he has never openly condemned the horrible excesses committed by his partisans, leaving a delirious press the task of pursuing a campaign against the Turks . . .

. . . The Turks at least are logical with themselves. They say, 'Life under these conditions is impossible. We are 120,000 menaced, in the full sense of the word, by extermination. There is but one solution: the partition of the island in two, we in the north, the Greeks in the south.' The Greeks are less frank. They deny the evidence . . .

. . . According to him [Archbishop Makarios] some changes in the constitution would be enough. The trouble is that these 'amendments' all tend to deprive the Turks of the rights and guarantees which had been accorded to them in 1960. The Turks reply: This amounts to saying to a drowning man 'Remove your life-belt and everything will be all right! . . .'

Appendix 3: *The Letter Sent by Archbishop Makarios to the President of the Greek Republic, General Phaedon Gizikis on 2 July 1974*

Nicosia, 2 July 1974.

Mr President,

It is with profound grief that I have to set out for you certain inadmissible situations and events in Cyprus for which I regard the Greek government responsible.

Since the clandestine arrival of General Grivas in Cyprus in September 1971, rumours have been circulating and there have been reliable indications that he came to Cyprus at the instigation and with the encouragement of certain circles in Athens. In any case, it is certain that from the first days of his arrival here, Grivas was in touch with officers from Greece serving in the National Guard from whom he received help and support in his effort to set up an unlawful organisation and allegedly to fight for Enosis. And he established the criminal EOKA 'B' organisation, which has become the cause and source of many sufferings for Cyprus. The activity of this organisation, which has committed political murders and many other crimes under a patriotic mantle advancing Enosis slogans, is well known. The National Guard, which is staffed and controlled by Greek officers, has been from the outset the main supplier of men and material to EOKA 'B', the members and supporters of which were euphemistically self-styled the 'Enosis camp'.

I have many times asked myself why an unlawful and nationally harmful organisation which is creating division and dissension, causing rifts in our internal front and leading the Greek Cypriot people to civil strife, is supported by Greek officers. And I have also many times wondered whether such support has the approval of the Greek government. I have done a great deal of thinking and made many hypothetical assumptions in order to find a logical reply to my questions. No reply, under any prerequisites and assumptions, could be based on logic. However, the Greek officers' support for EOKA 'B' constitutes an undeniable reality. The National Guard camps in various areas of the island and nearby sites are smeared with slogans in favour of Grivas and EOKA 'B' and also with slogans against the Cyprus government and particularly myself. In the National Guard camps, propaganda by Greek officers in favour of EOKA 'B' is often undisguised. It is also known, and an undeniable fact, that the opposition Cypriot press, which supports the criminal activity of EOKA 'B' and which has its sources of finance in Athens, receives guidance and direction from those in charge of the 2nd General Staff Office and the branch of the Greek Central Intelligence Service in Cyprus.

It is true that frequent complaints were conveyed by me to the Greek Government about the attitude and conduct of certain officers, and I have received the reply that I should not hesitate to report them by name and state the specific charges against them so that they could be recalled from Cyprus. I did this only in one instance. This is an unpleasant task for me. Moreover, this evil cannot be remedied by such means. What is important is the uprooting and prevention of the evil and not merely the facing of its consequences.

I am sorry to say, Mr President, that the root of the evil is very deep, reaching as far as Athens. It is from there that the tree of evil, the bitter fruits of which the Greek Cypriot people are tasting today, is being fed and maintained and helped to grow and spread. In order to be absolutely clear, I say that cadres of the Greek military regime support and direct the activities of the EOKA 'B' terrorist organisation. This explains also the involvement of Greek officers of the National Guard in illegal activities and in conspiratorial and other inadmissible situations. The guilt of the circles of the military regime is proved by documents which were found recently in the possession of leading cadres of EOKA 'B'. Plenty of money was sent from the National Centre for the maintenance of the organisation and directives were given concerning the leadership after the death of Grivas and the recall of Major Karousos, who had come to Cyprus with him, and generally everything was directed from Athens. The genuineness of the documents cannot be called into question because even those which are typewritten have corrections made by hand and the handwriting of the writer is known. I attach one such document.

I have always adhered to the principle, and I have on many occasions stated, that my co-operation with the Greek government for the time being is for me a national duty. The national interest dictates harmonious and close co-operation between Athens and Nicosia. No matter what Greek government was in power it was to me the government of the mother country and I had to co-operate with it. I cannot say that I have a special liking for military regimes, particularly in Greece the birthplace and cradle of democracy. But even in this case, I have not departed from my principle about co-operation. You realise, Mr President, the sad thoughts which have been preoccupying and tormenting me since ascertaining that men of the Greek government are incessantly hatching conspiracies against me and, what is worse, are dividing the Greek Cypriot people and pushing them towards catastrophe through civil strife. I have more than once so far felt, and in some cases I have almost touched, a hand invisibly extending from Athens and seeking to liquidate my human existence. For the sake of national expediency, however, I kept silent. Even the evil spirit which possessed the three defrocked Cypriot bishops who have caused a major crisis in the Church emanated from Athens. However, I said nothing in this connection. I am wondering what the object of all this is. I would have continued to keep silent about the responsibility and role of the Greek government in the present drama of Cyprus if I had been the only one to suffer on the scene of the drama. But covering things up and keeping silent is not permissible when the entire Greek Cypriot people are suffering, when Greek officers of the National Guard, at the instigation of Athens, support EOKA 'B' in its criminal activity, including political murders and generally aiming at the dissolution of the state.

The Greek government must take great responsibility for this attempt to abolish the state of Cyprus. The Cyprus state could be dissolved only in the event of Enosis. However, as long as Enosis is not feasible it is imperative that Cyprus should be strengthened as a state. By its whole attitude towards the National Guard issue, the Greek government has been following a policy calculated to abolish the Cyprus state.

A few months ago the National Guard General Staff, consisting of Greek officers, submitted to the Cyprus government for approval a list of candidates for cadet reserve officers during their military service. Fifty-seven of the candidates on the list submitted were not approved by the Council of Ministers. The General Staff was informed of this in writing. Despite this the General Staff, following instructions from Athens, paid no attention to the decision of the Council of Ministers which has the absolute right to appoint National Guard officers. Acting arbitrarily, the General Staff trampled upon laws, showed contempt for the decision of the Cyprus government and enrolled the candidates who had not been approved in the Officers Training School. I regard this attitude of the National Guard General Staff, which is controlled by the Greek government, as absolutely inadmissible. The National Guard is an organ of the Cyprus state and should be controlled by it and not from Athens. The theory about a common area of defence between Greece and Cyprus has its emotional aspect. In reality, however, the position is different. The National Guard, with its present composition and staffing, has deviated from its aim and has become a breeding ground for illegal activities, a centre of conspiracies against the state and a source of recruitment for EOKA 'B'. It suffices to say that during the recently stepped up terrorist activity of EOKA 'B', National Guard vehicles transported arms and moved to safety members of the organition who were about to be arrested. Complete responsibility for this improper conduct of the National Guard rests with Greek officers, some of whom are involved head over ears in the activities of EOKA 'B'. And the National Centre is not free from responsibility in this connection. The Greek government could by a mere nod put an end to this regrettable situation. The National Centre could order the termination of violence and terrorism by EOKA 'B' because it is from Athens that the organisation derives the means for its maintenance and its strength, as confirmed by written evidence and proof. The Greek government, however, has failed to do so. As an illustration of the inadmissible situation I note here in passing that in Athens slogans were also recently written against me and in favour of EOKA 'B' on the walls of churches and other buildings, including the building of the Cyprus Embassy. They did not seek to arrest and punish anybody, thus tolerating propaganda in favour of EOKA 'B'.

I have a lot to say, Mr President, but I do not think that I should say any more now. In conclusion, I convey that the Greek-officered National Guard, the plight of which has shaken the Cypriot people's confidence in it, will be restructured on a new basis. I have reduced military service so that the National Guard ceiling may be reduced and the extent of the evil may be limited. It may be observed that the reduction of the National Guard's strength by the shortening of military service, would render it incapable of carrying out its mission in the face of national danger. For reasons which I do not wish to set out here I do not share this view. And I would ask that the Greek officers staffing the National Guard be recalled. Their remaining in the National Guard and commanding the force would be harmful to relations between Athens and Nicosia. I would, however, be happy if you were to send to Cyprus about 100 officers as instructors and military advisers to help in the reorganisation and restructuring of the armed forces of Cyprus. I hope, in the meantime, that instructions have been given to EOKA 'B' to end its activities, even though, as long as this organisation is not definitely dissolved, a new wave of violence and murders cannot be ruled out.

I am sorry, Mr President, that I have found it necessary to say many unpleasant things in order to give a broad outline in open and frank terms of the long-standing, deplorable situation in Cyprus. This is, however, necessitated by the national interest which has always guided all my actions. I do not desire my co-operation with the Greek government to be interrupted. But it should be borne in mind that I am not an appointed prefect or locum tenens of the Greek government in Cyprus, but an elected leader of a large section of Hellenism and as such I demand an appropriate conduct by the National Centre towards me.

The content of this letter is not confidential.

With cordial wishes,
ARCHBISHOP MAKARIOS
President

Based on a translation published by the *Sunday Times*, 21 July 1974.

Appendix 4: *The Address Made by Archbishop Makarios before the UN Security Council on 19 July 1974 following the 15 July Coup (Security Council Official Records, S/PV.1780)*

PRESIDENT MAKARIOS: I should like at the outset to express my warmest thanks to the members of the Security Council for the keen interest they have shown in the critical situation created in Cyprus after the coup which was organised by the military regime of Greece and was put into effect by the Greek officers serving in and commanding the Cyprus National Guard. I am particularly grateful that the Security Council has agreed to postpone its meeting until my arrival here to give me the opportunity of addressing it on the recent dramatic events in Cyprus.

What has been happening in Cyprus since last Monday morning is a real tragedy. The military regime of Greece has callously violated the independence of Cyprus. Without trace of respect for the democratic rights of the Cypriot people, without trace of respect for the independence and sovereignty of the Republic of Cyprus, the Greek junta has extended its dictatorship to Cyprus. It is indeed a fact that for some time now their intention was becoming obvious. The people of Cyprus had for a long time the feeling that a coup by the Greek junta was brewing, and this feeling became more intense during the recent weeks when the terrorist organisation 'EOKA B', directed from Athens, had renewed its wave of violence. I knew all along that that illegal organisation had its roots and supply resources in Athens. I became aware that the Greek officers staffing and commanding the National Guard were recruiting members for that organisation, and they supported it in various ways to the point of access to the munition supply stores of the National Guard. In the camps of the National Guard, the Greek officers were conducting open propaganda in favour of that illegal organisation and turned the National Guard from an organ of the State into an instrument of subversion. Whenever, from time to time, I complained to Athens about unbecoming conduct by Greek officers of the National Guard, the reply was that if I had concrete evidence in proof thereof those found guilty would be recalled. From the whole tenor of their attitude, I received the unmistakable impression that their standard response was a pretence of innocence. A few days ago documents came into the hands of the Cyprus police clearly proving that 'EOKA B' was an appendage of the Athens regime.

Funds were being remitted from Athens for the upkeep of this organisation and detailed directives regarding its actions were also given to it. I then found it necessary myself to address a letter to the President of the Greek regime, General Gizikis, asking him to give orders for the cessation of the violence and bloodshed by 'EOKA B' and for its dissolution. I also requested him to recall the Greek officers serving with the National Guard, adding that my intention was to reduce the numerical strength of this Force and to turn it into an organ of the Cyprus State. I was waiting for a reply. My impression was that the Athens regime did not favour the reduction of the Force, much less the withdrawal of the Greek officers.

The Greek Ambassador in Cyprus called on me, on instructions from his Government, in order to explain to me that the decrease in the numerical strength of the National Guard or the withdrawal of the Greek officers would weaken the defence of Cyprus in case of danger from Turkey. This was an argument which, even though it appeared logical, was not convincing because I knew that behind this argument other interests were hidden. I replied that as things developed I consider the danger from Turkey of a lesser degree than the danger from them. And it was proved that my fears were justified.

On Saturday, 13 July, a conference under the presidency of General Gizikis was held in Athens which lasted for many hours. It was attended by the Greek Chief of Staff of the armed forces, the Ambassador of Greece to Cyprus, the Commander of the National Guard and other officials, for the purpose of discussing the content of my letter. As was stated in a relevant communiqué issued at the end of this conference, it was to be reconvened on Monday, 15 July. The reference in the communiqué to a second conference was deceiving. For while on Monday I was waiting for a reply to my letter the reply came, and it was the coup.

On that day, I returned from my summer house on the Troodos mountains, where I had spent the week-end, and by 8 a.m. I was at my office at the Presidential Palace. Half an hour later I was welcoming in the reception room a group of boys and girls, members of the Greek Orthodox Youth from Cairo who came to Cyprus as my guests for a few days. Hardly had I greeted them when the first shots were heard. Within seconds the shots became more frequent and a member of the Presidential Guard informed me that armoured cars and tanks had passed the fence and were already in the yard of the Presidential Palace which was shaking from mortar shells. The situation soon became critical. I tried to call the Cyprus Radio Station for the purpose of issuing a special broadcast announcing that the Presidential Palace was under attack, but I realised that the lines were cut off. Heavy shelling was ever increasing. How my life was saved seemed like a providential miracle. When I eventually found myself in the area of Paphos, I addressed the people of Cyprus from a local radio station informing them that I am alive and that I will struggle with them against the dictatorship which the Greek regime is trying to impose.

I do not intend to occupy the time of the members of the Security Council with my personal adventure. I simply wish to add that during the second day of the armed attack the armoured cars and tanks were moving towards Paphos, while at the same time a small warship of the National Guard began shelling the Bishophric of Paphos where I was staying. Under the circumstances, I found it advisable to leave Cyprus rather than fall into the hands of the Greek junta.

I am grateful to the British Government which made available a helicopter to pick me up from Paphos, transfer me to the British bases, and from there by plane to Malta and London. I am also grateful to the Special Representative of the Secretary-General and to the Commander of the Peace-Keeping Force in Cyprus for the interest which they had shown for my safety. My presence in this room of the Security Council was made possible thanks to the help given to me by the British Government and the representatives of the Secretary-General, Dr Waldheim, whose keen concern for me and for the critical situation which developed in Cyprus moves every fibre of my heart.

I do not know as yet all the details of the Cyprus crisis caused by the Greek military regime. I am afraid that the number of casualties is large and that the material destruction is heavy. What is, however, our primary concern at present is the ending of the tragedy.

When I reached London, I was informed of the content of

the speech of the representative of the Greek junta to the United Nations. I was surprised at the way they are trying to deceive world public opinion. Without a blush, the Greek junta is making efforts to simplify the situation, claiming that it is not involved in the armed attack and that the developments of the last few days are an internal matter of the Greek Cypriots.

I do not believe that there are people who accept the allegations of the Greek military regime. The coup did not come about under such circumstances as to be considered an internal matter of the Greek Cypriots. It is clearly an invasion from outside, in flagrant violation of the independence and sovereignty of the Republic of Cyprus. The so-called coup was the work of the Greek officers staffing and commanding the National Guard. I must also underline the fact that the Greek contingent, composed of 950 officers and men stationed in Cyprus by virtue of the Treaty of Alliance, played a predominant role in this aggressive affair against Cyprus. The capture of the airport outside the capital was carried out by officers and men of the Greek contingent camping near the airport.

It is enough to state on this point that certain photographs appearing in the world press show armoured vehicles and tanks belonging to the Greek contingent in Cyprus. On the other hand, the Greek officers serving with the National Guard were directing the operations. In these operations, they recruited many members of the terrorist organisation 'EOKA B', whom they armed with weapons of the National Guard.

If the Greek officers serving in the National Guard were not involved, how does one explain the fact that among the casualties in battle were Greek officers whose remains were transported to Greece and buried there? If Greek officers did not carry out the coup, how does one explain the fact of night flights of Greek aircraft transporting to Cyprus personnel in civilian clothes and taking back to Greece dead and wounded men? There is no doubt that the coup was organised by the Greek junta and was carried out by the Greek officers commanding the National Guard and by the officers and men of the Greek contingent stationed in Cyprus – and it was reported as such by the press around the globe.

The coup caused much bloodshed and took a great toll of human lives. It was faced with the determined resistance of the legal security forces and the resistance of the Greek people of Cyprus. I can say with certainty that the resistance and the reaction of the Greek Cypriot people against the conspirators will not end until there is a restoration of their freedom and democratic rights. The Cypriot people will never bow to dictatorship, even though for the moment the brutal force of the armoured cars and tanks may have prevailed.

After the coup the agents of the Greek regime in Cyprus appointed a well-known gun-man, Nicos Sampson, as President, who in turn appointed as ministers known elements and supporters of the terrorist organisation 'EOKA B'.

It may be alleged that what took place in Cyprus is a revolution and that a Government was established based on revolutionary law. This is not the case. No revolution took place in Cyprus which could be considered as an internal matter. It was an invasion, which violated the independence and the sovereignty of the Republic. And the invasion is continuing so long as there are Greek officers in Cyprus. The results of this invasion will be catalytic for Cyprus if there is no return to constitutional normality and if democratic freedoms are not restored.

For the purpose of misleading world public opinion, the military regime of Greece announced yesterday the gradual replacement of the Greek officers of the National Guard. But the issue is not their replacement; the issue is their withdrawal. The gesture of replacement has the meaning of admission that the Greek officers now serving in the National Guard were those who carried out the coup. Those officers, however, did not act on their own initiative but upon instructions from Athens, and their replacements will also follow instructions from the Athens regime. Thus the National Guard will always remain an instrument of the Greek military regime, and I am certain that the members of the Security Council understand this ploy.

It may be said that it was the Cyprus Government which invited the Greek officers to staff the National Guard. I regret to say that it was a mistake on my part to bestow upon them so much trust and confidence. They abused that trust and confidence and, instead of helping in the defence of the Island's independence, sovereignty and territorial integrity, they themselves became the aggressors.

I am obliged to say that the policy of the military regime in Greece towards Cyprus, and particularly towards the Greek Cypriots, has been insincere. I wish to stress that it was a policy of duplicity.

For some time talks were going on between the Greek and Turkish Cypriots in search of a peaceful solution to the Cyprus problem, which on many occasions has occupied the time of the Security Council and the General Assembly of the United Nations. The representative of the Secretary-General and two constitutional experts from Greece and Turkey have been attending the talks. The Security Council has repeatedly renewed, twice yearly, the mandate of the peace-keeping Force in Cyprus, expressing every time hope for a speedy solution of the problem.

It cannot be said that up to now the progress of the talks has been satisfactory. But how could there be any progress in the talks while the policy on Cyprus of the regime in Athens has been double-faced? It was agreed by all the parties concerned that the talks were taking place on the basis of independence. The regime of Athens also agreed to that, and time and again the Greek Ministry of Foreign Affairs declared that the position of Greece on this issue was clear. If that were the case, why had the military regime of Greece created and supported the terrorist organisation 'EOKA B', whose purpose was stated to be the union of Cyprus with Greece and whose members called themselves 'unionists'?

Inside the camps of the National Guard, the Greek officers continually charged that while *Enosis* was feasible its realisation was undermined by me. When reminded that Greece had made its position clear on this and that it supported independence, their reply was that no attention should be given to the words of diplomats. Under such circumstances how was it possible for the talks to arrive at a positive result? The double-faced policy of the Greek regime was one of the main obstacles to the progress of the talks.

In the circumstances that have now been created in Cyprus, I cannot foresee the prospects of the talks. I would rather say that there are no prospects at all. An agreement that may be reached by the talks would be devoid of any value because there is no elected leadership to deal with the matter. The coup d'état of the military regime of Greece constitutes an arrest of the progress of the talks towards a solution. Moreover, it will be a continuous source of anomaly in Cyprus, the repercussions of which will be very grave and far-reaching, if this situation is permitted to continue even for a short time.

I appeal to the members of the Security Council to do their utmost to put an end to this anomalous situation which was created by the coup of Athens. I call upon the Security Council to use all ways and means at its disposal so that the constitutional order in Cyprus and the democratic rights of the people of Cyprus can be reinstated without delay.

As I have already stated, the events in Cyprus do not constitute an internal matter of the Greeks of Cyprus. The

Turks of Cyprus are also affected. The coup of the Greek junta is an invasion, and from its consequences the whole people of Cyprus suffers, both Greeks and Turks. The United Nations has a peace-keeping Force stationed in Cyprus. It is not possible for the role of that peace-keeping Force to be effective under conditions of a military coup. The Security Council should call upon the military regime of Greece to withdraw from Cyprus the Greek officers serving in the National Guard, and to put an end to its invasion of Cyprus.

I think that, with what I have placed before you, I have given a picture of the situation. I have no doubt that an appropriate decision of the Security Council will put an end to the invasion and restore the violated independence of Cyprus and the democratic rights of the Cypriot people.

Appendix 5: *The Report of the UN Secretary-General No. S/12323 of 30 April 1977, Pursuant to Paragraph 6 of Security Council Resolution 401 (1976)*

(1) In operative paragraph 6 of its resolution 401 (1976) of 14 December 1976, the Security Council requested me 'to continue the mission of good offices entrusted to [me] by paragraph 6 of resolution 367 (1975) to keep the Security Council informed of the progress made and to submit a report on the implementation of this resolution by 30 April 1977'. After the adoption of that resolution, I assured the Council that I would continue my efforts to bring about a resumption of the negotiations between the representatives of the two Cypriot communities at an early date, and that I and my Special Representative would be making contact with the parties concerned with a view to ensuring that such negotiations would be meaningful and would concern themselves with the basic issues of the Cyprus problem (S/PV. 1979).

(2) On 11 January 1977, His Excellency Mr Rauf Denktash requested my Special Representative to transmit to His Beatitude Archbishop Makarios a letter dated 9 January, expressing Mr Denktash's readiness to meet with the archbishop in the presence of the Special Representative

with a view to settling the basic approach to the Cyprus problem. Mr Denktash also handed to Mr Perez de Cuéllar, for transmission, a letter on the same subject addressed to me.

(3) The reply of Archbishop Makarios to Mr Denktash's letter, conveyed orally through my Special Representative, was positive and the meeting was held in the latter's presence at UNFICYP headquarters on 27 January 1977. After the meeting each of the two leaders made public statements to the effect that the meeting had been useful to both sides and held in a friendly atmosphere, but that there was need for clarification on a great number of points, some of which had been discussed.

(4) The desirability of a further high-level meeting under my personal auspices was evoked during the 27 January meeting and it was agreed to schedule such a meeting to coincide with the end of my visit to countries in the Middle East. I arrived in Cyprus on 12 February and met with the two leaders on the same day at UNFICYP headquarters. The following statement was issued:

> During our talks, which lasted for four hours, instructions have been worked out for the representatives in the inter-communal talks as the basis for future negotiations.
>
> It has also been agreed to reconvene the Cyprus talks in Vienna under the auspices of the Secretary-General at the end of March.

(5) The text of the agreed instructions (guidelines) referred to in the above communiqué reads as follows:

(1) We are seeking an independent, non-aligned, bi-communal Federal Republic.
(2) The territory under the administration of each community should be discussed in the light of economic viability or productivity and land ownership.

(3) Questions of principles like freedom of movement, freedom of settlement, the right of property and other specific matters, are open for discussion taking into consideration the fundamental basis of a bi-communal federal system and certain practical difficulties which may arise for the Turkish Cypriot community.

(4) The powers and functions of the Central Federal Government will be such as to safeguard the unity of the country, having regard to the bi-communal character of the State.

(6) During the next few weeks intensive preparatory talks were conducted with all concerned in the light of the above guidelines. My efforts and those of my Special Representative in that connection were also supported by diplomatic initiatives undertaken by a number of Governments. I was kept fully informed about those initiatives. On 8 March it was announced that the intercommunal talks would reconvene in Vienna under my auspices on 31 March and that, after my scheduled departure on 4 April, I would continue to be represented at the talks by my Special Representative.

(7) The new series of talks began in Vienna as scheduled on 31 March. I opened the first meeting, which began in public, with a statement, the text of which is reproduced in Annex A [see p. 161 below]. The talks then continued in private. After the last meeting on 7 April, the following communiqué was issued:

> The first round of the new series of intercommunal talks was held in Vienna from 31 March to 7 April 1977. The first five meetings were held under the personal auspices of the Secretary-General. Following the Secretary-General's scheduled departure from Vienna on 4 April, six more meetings were held under the auspices of his Special Representative in Cyprus, Mr Javier Perez de Cuéllar.

The interlocutors initiated the discussion of the Cyprus problem, including the specific questions of principle, within the framework of the guidelines agreed upon at the high-level meeting held in Nicosia on 12 February 1977 in the presence of the Secretary-General.

Proposals were submitted on the territorial aspect by the representative of the Greek Cypriot community, and on the constitutional aspect by the representative of the Turkish Cypriot community. These proposals were discussed and certain clarifications were made.

It has not been possible to bridge the considerable gap between the views of the two sides. Efforts will be continued to overcome the differences. To this end, it was agreed that the talks will resume in Nicosia about the middle of May 1977 under the auspices of the Special Representative of the Secretary-General in preparation for a further round in Vienna.

(8) The first round of the new series of talks, concluded on 7 April, was the longest of all the sessions held under my auspices since the adoption of resolution 367 (1975), and the substantive aspects of the Cyprus problem were discussed at some length.

(9) For the first time, the Greek Cypriot side submitted a specific territorial proposal together with a map embodying its conception of a bi-communal arrangement (Annex B) [not included]. The proposal was made subject to certain principles, including the preservation of the sovereignty and unity of the Republic and of the rights of the freedom of movement, residence, work and property of all citizens (Annex C) [not included].

(10) For its part, the Turkish Cypriot side submitted a constitutional proposal (Annex D) [not included] calling for a partnership in power between two equal political entities joining their resources in a federal administration on

a basis of equality, working together at first in a comparatively limited field. The functions proposed for the Federal Government would be expected to grow, a process described by the Turkish Cypriot representative as 'federation by evolution'.

(11) Each interlocutor made it clear that his own proposals were negotiable. However, each emphasised certain principles conflicting with those of the other side, and each commented negatively on the proposals submitted by the other.

(12) The Greek Cypriot side contended that the Turkish Cypriot constitutional plan would be in effect a treaty between independent entities, providing not for a federal government but for a confederal system without powers, which could only evolve, if at all, in the direction of complete separation. Since it considered the Turkish Cypriot proposal to be based on unacceptable premises, the Greek Cypriot side felt unable to propose amendments to it, and instead submitted a document of its own on the subject (Annex E) [not included].

(13) The Turkish Cypriot side contended that the Greek Cypriot territorial proposal was not a bi-zonal one, that it failed to take account of the requirements of economic viability or productivity, that it would deprive the Turkish Cypriot community of vital resources and would jeopardise its security. The Turkish Cypriot interlocutor, while not accepting the Greek Cypriot proposal, emphasised that he was in no position, and was not expected, to submit a territorial counter-proposal or draw a line of his own on the map. As for the Greek Cypriot constitutional document, the Turkish Cypriot side considered that this would create a unitary rather than federal state, and was therefore unacceptable.

(14) In my opening statement on 31 March, I reminded the interlocutors that it was my understanding that each side would be prepared to negotiate the proposals submitted

by the other in a substantive way with a view to reconciling the present differences in their positions. However, in spite of my own efforts and those of my Special Representative, it did not prove possible in Vienna to reach a stage where an effective negotiating process could evolve out of the present statements of conflicting positions. On the other hand, and as stated in the agreed communiqué of 7 April, there was some discussion of the respective proposals and a number of clarifications were made. These points will of course be pursued when the talks resume. There is evidently still a long way to go in order to reach the point where the necessary concessions will begin to be made, including the submission of substantive proposals on both main aspects of the problem. For this it will be necessary for both sides to make vastly increased efforts to appreciate one another's positions, apprehensions and aspirations.

(15) I and my Special Representative are determined to pursue our efforts to move the current negotiating process into a more constructive phase. I hope that future political developments will assist the parties in bridging the conceptual and substantive differences that separate them. My Special Representative is currently engaged in contacts with both sides in Cyprus in preparation for the resumption of the talks in Nicosia. I shall continue to keep the Security Council informed of developments in this regard.

ANNEX A: OPENING STATEMENT BY THE SECRETARY-GENERAL AT THE CYPRUS TALKS IN VIENNA 31 MARCH 1977

Distinguished representatives,
    I take great pleasure in welcoming you once again in Vienna and in opening formally the first meeting of the new series of the intercommunal talks.

We have come a long way since we met for consultations in New York last September. The meetings that brought together His Beatitude Archbishop Makarios and His Excellency Mr Denktash in Nicosia, first in the presence of my Special Representative, Mr Perez de Cuéllar, and then on 12 February under my auspices, have changed the political atmosphere surrounding negotiations on the Cyprus question. I wish to take this opportunity to pay a warm tribute once again to the two leaders, both of whom made great efforts and, by these efforts, overcame many of the difficulties which stood in the way of resuming the negotiating process.

As I indicated in Nicosia in February, I consider that we have now reached a point where meaningful negotiations on the various aspects of the Cyprus problem should become possible. The basic elements of such negotiations are contained in the four guidelines which the two leaders agreed upon last month and which have been entrusted for implementation to the interlocutors now present at this table.

These guidelines cover the principal aspects of an agreed, peaceful, durable and just solution of the Cyprus problem. They include, as we all know, the territorial and constitutional issues. It is my understanding that both sides are agreed to discuss all of these aspects during the forthcoming meetings. It is further agreed by all concerned that a solution of these very complex problems must of necessity result in a package deal, and that therefore an agreement on any one item would only become final in the framework of agreement on all.

It is also my understanding that each side will be prepared to negotiate the proposals submitted by the other in a substantive way with a view to reconciling the present differences in the positions of the two sides. Indeed, I am convinced that this is the only basis on which we can hope to make concrete progress.

These meetings in Vienna will go on until 7 April. After that, talks will continue in Nicosia in order to take up various points in greater detail prior to a further round in Vienna. It is essential that we now embark on a continuous and progressive process of negotiation with the ultimate objective of an agreed settlement of the Cyprus problem. I have no illusions about the difficulties of this task, but I am convinced this is far the best available means of making real progress.

The guidelines agreed upon on 12 February provide us with a sound basis for a new and determined effort. I hope that in the meetings here we shall be able to make significant steps forward towards an agreed settlement. Obviously this will be a long and arduous process, in which we cannot expect quick results. What we have to do here is to launch a process of meaningful and substantive negotiation which will enable us to establish the framework of an agreement within a reasonable time.

This is a crucial moment. I therefore appeal to both sides to make a determined effort to narrow the gap between their positions. It is clear to me, and I am sure to all concerned, that there is no viable alternative to a mutually acceptable solution for the Cyprus problem. The time to negotiate such a solution is now. For the good of all the people of Cyprus, and for the sake of the broader peace, I hope that we will seize the opportunity which is now presented to us.

Appendix 6: *The Testimony of the Greek Cypriot Priest, Papatsestos, as Published in Local Greek Newspapers on 28 February 1976*

PAPATSESTOS: Two days after the coup, on 17 July, I witnessed something which has perhaps never been witnessed by any mortal before. I saw a young Greek Cypriot buried alive. That was when two Junta officers came to my house and ordered me to accompany them to the cemetery. I thought they were going to kill me, but they said they only wanted me for burying some dead people.

In the cemetery there were two open graves and two bodies lying beside them. I went to see if I could recognise them. One was dead. But the other, a curly-haired, fair-complexioned, 18-year-old youth, was moving. Startled, I turned back and shouted: 'But officer, this man is alive!'

'Shut up you dirty priest, or I will shut you up for good', the officer retorted. Then the youth was pushed into the open grave which was filled with earth. I swear to God that they buried this youth while he was still alive!

[Pointing at the cemetery, Papatsestos said]

Here people were buried like dogs by the Junta. There were also bodies which had been dumped outside the cemetery. They were not identified, and not claimed. As a priest my conscience is troubled, but they were holding a pistol to my head at the time.

I remember the day they first came to me. They said 'Father, we have some dead bodies which we want you to bury'. 'Certainly', I replied and asked how many bodies they had. Seventy-seven they said. An hour later a lorry arrived and I heard someone order: 'Dump them outside.' They were the dead bodies; they were all put in one common grave, without waiting for identification by their relatives. The Junta men produced some small crosses (seven only!), wrote some names on them and put them on the grave.

The Junta men scornfully called persons loyal to Makarios 'Muskos supporters', and wanted to bury them 'like dogs', in a sheep-fold outside the cemetery. And that is what they did in the end. They dug two graves with excavators – one inside and the other outside the cemetery. They buried their own dead (27) inside the cemetery and others (5) outside.

TA NEA: Father, about the young man buried alive, could he have been saved?

PAPATSESTOS: Of course he could have been saved. He had a wound in the right leg. I went to the hospital and asked a doctor there, if a dead man could move. The doctor laughed, and said 'No'. But I was not the one who had buried him alive.

TA NEA: Could you recognise any of the Junta men?

PAPATSESTOS:	They had all come from Greece for the coup. They were looting, and they even broke into my house. They entered houses on the pretext of searching for deserters but actually stole valuable articles from them.
TA NEA:	Have you witnessed any other atrocities?
PAPATSESTOS:	I listened to telephone conversations between Junta men. In one case they were talking about the people resisting at Kaimakli suburb, and saying: 'Shoot them all, have no mercy at all!' I also noticed that in the hospital they were giving polluted water to the sick.
TA NEA:	Father, could you swear that you have not secretly buried dead Turks in the cemetery?
PAPATSESTOS:	Only about 10. We did not know who they were and where they were found.
TA NEA:	How many bodies did you bury during the coup?
PAPATSESTOS:	127. Fifty of them were collected from the streets and they were buried outside the cemetery; the other 77 were buried inside.
TA NEA:	If the Turkish invasion had not taken place, would more Greek Cypriots have been killed in the coup?
PAPATSESTOS:	Oh yes, many more. They wanted to kill me too. It is rather a hard thing to say, but it is true, that the Turkish intervention saved us from a merciless internecine war. They had prepared a list of all Makarios supporters and they would have slaughtered them all.
TA NEA:	Now, father tell me sincerely, were people brutally killed in those days?
PAPATSESTOS:	Yes, my son. Massacres were committed outside Kykko Monastery and in Limassol.

147

> I heard with my own ears the order. *'All of them, to the last man, must be killed tonight.'*
>
> Those who have witnessed these crimes are afraid to speak. As a matter of fact most of them are Grivas supporters and they will never speak.

Finally, Papatsestos is reported to have declared that he would tell his story and worries to the Greek Premier, Mr Constantine Karamanlis, because Makarios has done nothing about them.

Appendix 7: Letter from Mr Tassos Papadopoullos of 26 April 1977 Rejecting the Turkish Cypriot Suggestion for Setting Up a Committee to Trace Missing Persons

Confidential

The gist of the Greek Cypriot proposals is that:

(a) The committee should be established on the lines of the suggestion of the ICRC already unofficially made (see Annex).

(b) The committee should be composed, in addition to UN and ICRC officials, of an equal number of Greek Cypriot and Turkish Cypriot representatives of the Cyprus Red Cross Society and by representatives of the Committee of Relatives of Missing Persons, Greek and Turkish Cypriots.

(c) Its powers and functions should be decided by the committee itself on the advice of the ICRC, but in any event it should have powers to collect, verify, analyse and follow through evidence on missing persons including powers of checking on any area under such conditions that might accommodate any Turkish security consideration.

(d) The Greek Cypriot side is prepared to agree that firm assurances should be given and concrete measures taken to ensure that no propaganda capital of any kind should be made by either side as to its work, functions or findings.

(e) As to the demand of the Turkish Cypriot side (reference para. 1(a) of Mr Denktash's document) that a public statement should be issued, the Greek Cypriot side agrees that a statement (not verbatim as suggested by Mr Denktash but to the effect that cases of Turkish Cypriot missing people will also be investigated) should be issued. Such a statement will be issued after the setting up of the committee and the agreement as to its composition, but not before. The Greek Cypriot and the Turkish Cypriot authorities must in the same statement pledge their unconditional co-operation in helping the investigation of these cases.

(f) The lists of missing persons will be exchanged at the first meeting of this investigatory committee.

(g) To allay any professed Turkish fears as to propaganda exploitation it is agreeable that no publicity whatsoever (other than the statement in clause (e) above) will be made and if any leakage to the press occurs there will immediately be a satisfactory official denial.

ANNEX

The ICRC might agree to designate or participate in the designation of members of an investigatory body which should include specialists in forensic medicine provided the following conditions are complied with:

(1) Both parties should make the request.

(2) Both parties should undertake to give their full co-

operation including freedom of movement throughout Cyprus, furnishing of all relevant information which may be required by the investigatory body.

(3) Both parties would agree in advance to accept as final the conclusions and recommendations of the investigatory body whether pertaining to the existence or not of missing persons and in the affirmative of measures to be taken in their respect.

(4) Suitable arrangements will be made for financing the operation.

The Minutes of the Discussion on Missing Persons between Archbishop Makarios and Mr Rauf Denktash at Meetings Held on 27 January and 12 February 1977 Released on 27 October 1977

(PRESS RELEASE FROM THE PUBLIC INFORMATION OFFICE OF THE TURKISH FEDERATED STATE OF CYPRUS ON 27 OCTOBER 1977)

The President of the Turkish Federated State of Cyprus, Mr Rauf Denktash, gave the following statement today to the Turkish radio and television correspondent in Nicosia on the question of the missing persons:

For the Greek Cypriot leaders the question of missing persons is nothing but subject for sheer propaganda. During the two meetings I had with Archbishop Makarios on 27 January and 12 February, he stated that he was obliged to keep this question alive for propaganda purposes. The following is the text of my conversation with Archbishop Makarios on this subject:

MAKARIOS: Mr Denktash, after this meeting with you the families of missing persons will again come to me and ask whether I discussed the issue with you. What shall I tell them?

DENKTASH: Tell them the truth. Stop exploiting this question for propaganda purposes. Do not deceive the suffering people by giving them false hopes. Why opt for propaganda rather than the truth?

MAKARIOS: I have no weapon left to me other than propaganda . . .

DENKTASH: Is it right that you should choose propaganda on this issue in spite of the facts? You are prolonging the suffering of the people. Tell them the truth.

MAKARIOS: But what facts can I give them?

DENKTASH: Do you know how many Greek Cypriots were killed during the coup and where they were buried?

MAKARIOS: No, I don't know.

DENKTASH: But you yourself are on record as having stated at the United Nations that the Junta had caused great bloodshed on the island. Don't you know the cost of life caused by this bloodshed?

MAKARIOS: I assure you that I do not know the number of people killed or missing during the coup.

DENKTASH: According to the Scandinavian press the number of dead exceeded 2,000. A letter written by a Greek Cypriot professor in London to a Turkish Cypriot (Mr Alper Orhon) in Nicosia, stated that he had seen hundreds of dead in the streets of Limassol. Our information confirms this. Then there is the statement by your own priest that appeared in your newspapers. The rebels were bringing the dead in lorryloads and were having them buried, including the ones who were still breathing, in mass graves. These are the facts. How can you ask me and Turkey to account for 2,000 Greek Cypriots without taking these facts into consideration? We examined these questions in depth with Mr Clerides. The International Red Cross also assisted us in our work. In the end only about thirty cases remain as 'pending'. It was also established at our meetings that all Greek Cypriot prisoners of war taken to Turkey had been returned to you. Of the 'pending' cases, which are about 30, we have already supplied information on the first 8 or 9 cases. If you like I shall repeat it here.

MAKARIOS: I know the subject. However, can't we form an investigation committee for these 23 to 24 outstanding cases?

DENKTASH: We can. The Turkish Cypriot Red Crescent representatives from our side and the Greek Cypriot Red Cross representatives from your side can come together and investigate these cases by obtaining the help of the families of missing persons. We can help them. However, before embarking on this I shall request certain things from you.

MAKARIOS: Please go ahead.

DENKTASH: You are looking for 23 or 24 missing persons. These persons became 'missing' during a war. We want to learn from you the fate of 203 Turkish Cypriots who were picked up from the roads and workplaces by Greek Cypriot policemen during 1963–4. Until 1968 the families of these Turkish Cypriots lived with the hope that you were keeping them as prisoners. When we started negotiations with Mr Clerides in 1968, the first thing I asked him was the fate of these people. He told me that they had all been killed. I acted differently from you on this issue. I told the families the bitter truth. Some fainted. However, they were relieved of expectation and suffering day after day, they adjusted their lives accordingly and they obtained their legal rights. They returned to normal life. The Greek Cypriot leadership has not made a formal announcement on this subject, yet. If you are going to start investigations about the fate of 23 or 24 missing Greek Cypriots, you must first of all tell us by whom these Turkish Cypriots were annihilated. You must disclose where they are. These people were killed by your policemen and elements you armed yourself and you must explain why these people were not brought to justice.

Again in 1963 you exterminated the whole Turkish Cypriot population, including the children and women, of the village of Ayios Vassilios in December 1963. The Red Cross found the bodies of 13 of them in mass graves. Where are the others? We shall expect an explanation from you about them.

In 1974, 113 Turkish Cypriots were picked up from their homes in Tokhni (Taskent), Mari Tatlisu), and Zyyi (Terazi) by your policemen and soldiers and taken away. These Turkish Cypriots were lined up and shot dead near Limassol. This was the fate that befell the 40 to 50 Turkish Cypriots that were in the first bus. We know this because one of them pretended to be dead after he was wounded and then escaped to the British Bases and has given us a statement. Mr Clerides has confessed that the passengers of the second bus met the same fate. I informed Mr Clerides about the leaders of these crimes. No investigations were initiated about anyone and you made no official statement about the incident. If you now want to start investigations about the fate of 23 to 24 Greek Cypriots, you must make an announcement as to who killed these Turkish Cypriots, why they were killed, and where their graves are. The question of missing Greek Cypriots is an issue that occurred during the war in 1974 and it involves 23 to 24 persons. Whereas the missing Turkish Cypriots were picked up from their homes and business places by your policemen and soldiers who took them away and never returned them.

Unless you account for these and clear yourself, we shall conclude that you are not seriously interested in the fate of 23 to 24 Greek Cypriots. The fact that you keep on talking about 2,000 missing Greek Cypriots in total disregard of the facts, proves that you are interested in nothing but propaganda.

As someone interested in missing persons, you should first of all investigate why and how hundreds of Turkish civilians were found in mass graves after being sought for months as missing persons. Turkish Cypriots listed for months as missing persons from Aloa (Atlilar), Maratha (Murataga), Sandallaris (Sandallar) and Paphos were found in mass graves. How and why were they killed? How can anyone ask us questions on such issues without fulfilling his own obligations? What is more, in spite of all this, we have furnished what we know about your people.

Appendix 9:

A Statement by the Chairman of the Committee of Relatives of Turkish Cypriot Missing Persons, Dr Oğuz Veli Beidoğlu, Rebutting Allegations made by Father Christoforos, Chairman of the Committee of Relatives of Greek Cypriot Missing Persons, on 18 July 1979

(PRESS RELEASE NO. 3 FROM THE PUBLIC INFORMATION OFFICE OF THE TURKISH FEDERATED STATE OF CYPRUS, 19 JULY 1979)

'This outcry of lament by a people who, for 16 years, refused to provide us with the slightest information about our own missing persons, is a simple propaganda gambit. We are also awaiting the establishment of the investigatory Committee, to be set up with the participation of the International Red Cross.

We would like to remind them that those who, in 1974, killed hundreds of unarmed Turks and buried them in mass graves, have not yet disclosed the names of the Greeks and Turks they killed during the coup.

Three years have gone by since the disclosure made by Papatsetsos describing how he had been compelled, at gunpoint, to bury truck-loads of dead men killed during the coup and dumped into mass graves. We have yet to be furnished with a list of the names of these unfortunate people.

The burial place of our kinsmen from Tokhni, Mari and Zyyi, taken as hostages in 1974 and shot before a firing squad somewhere near Limassol, has also not been disclosed.

From the point of view of world public opinion, it is indeed shameful that these people, these Greek Cypriot leaders with such a horrid past, should turn the question of missing persons into an instrument of inhuman propaganda. We strongly protest at this deplorable approach.

On behalf of the families of Turkish Cypriot missing persons, I would like to reiterate that we are not against the establishment of an investigatory committee, to be set up with the participation of a representative of the International Red Cross, to commence its investigations for the purpose of solving the question of missing persons, beginning with Turkish Cypriot missing persons, that is to say with missing persons who disappeared during 1963-8; but we are against the insistent proposition of Greek Cypriots who, for propaganda purposes, demand that a representative of the UN Secretary-General, whose involvement in politics would be inevitable, should be substituted, in the said committee, in place of the representative of the International Red Cross.

It will be recalled that during the years 1974-5 the International Committee of the Red Cross, having investigated the question of missing persons through a joint committee of Greeks and Turks:

(a) had reaffirmed that all Greek Cypriot prisoners taken to Turkey had been handed over to the Greek side;
(b) had established that a good number of people alleged

to be missing were actually alive and residing on the Greek side;

(c) had notified the two sides about its findings concerning a great number of missing persons whose files had been closed; and

(d) had closed its local bureau after handing over to the then interlocutors – Messrs Denktash and Clerides – some 30 files pending finalisation of investigations.

It is because they know they will not be able to use the ICRC as an instrument in their ugly and inhuman propaganda that the Greeks are opposing this organisation.

We invite the attention of world public opinion to these stark realities.

Greek Cypriot leaders have no right or authority to mock at the sentiments of sorrow-stricken people.

We call upon the Government of the Turkish Federated State of Cyprus to accept no other formula than the resolution unanimously adopted in 1977 in the Third Committee of the UN General Assembly; and to insist that as previously agreed the necessary investigations should be carried out in chronological sequence.'

Appendix 10: *Address Made by Mr Rauf Denktash before the Security Council, during its Cyprus Debate on 27 November 1978*

DENKTASH: I thank you, Mr President, and the members of the Council for having given me this opportunity to make a statement on behalf of the Turkish Cypriots of Cyprus, who were the partner co-founders of the Republic of Cyprus, which was subjected to attacks by Greek Cypriots as far back as in 1963. That destruction has continued until today, and the co-founder partner community of the island has to take such opportunities as may be given to it, through your indulgence Mr President and members of the Council, in order to make its case known to the highest body of this world Assembly.

If I cannot promise to be brief, it is not because of disrespect to you, Sir, and it is not because I am not aware of the hours of frustration which you have spent in trying to bring about an agreement so that these proceedings might go forward speedily. Quite the contrary. It is because I feel that the Turkish-Cypriot case has to be restated with vigour, within reason, so that what might follow from now onwards will not be considered to be the responsibility of the Turkish Cypriot community, which has throughout its life in Cyprus, throughout its struggle in Cyprus, done nothing other than react to what the Greek Cypriots tried to do to Cyprus.

I should like to refer to the statement made to the Council by Mr Rolandis on 15 November when he said:

'In Cyprus . . . there is room only for resistance against injustice and brutality' (S/PV.2099, p. 3).

He launched a bitter attack on the representative of Turkey and alleged that there was no Cyprus Government. Well, that statement that there is no Cyprus Government affects the co-founder partner community of the legitimate Government of Cyprus which, I say on behalf of the Turkish Cypriot community, ceased to exist as a legitimate Government on the 21st day of December 1963 when the Greek Cypriots attacked us, when they threw the Turkish Cypriot community out of the Government and they rejected the Turkish Cypriot community as a co-founder partner community and continue to reject us to this very day.

I join the voice of the representative of Turkey in repeating before the Council that if there is a Cyprus problem today it is because there is no Government by consent in Cyprus. One-fourth of the population of Cyprus is not under the jurisdiction of an administration which calls itself the Government of Cyprus but which has nothing to do with the bi-national Government envisaged in the 1960 international agreements. The Greek section of this bi-national Government armed itself and, in accordance with a plan, attacked the Turkish community with a view to Hellenising Cyprus. After 15 years, after all the trials and tribulations of Cyprus, we heard them speak in the General Assembly, later in the Special Political Committee and still later in the Security Council, for and on behalf of Cyprus and attempt to speak for and on behalf of the Turkish Cypriots.

If the United Nations Charter stands for democracy, if it stands for Government under the rule of law, if it stands for Governments with the sanction of the governed, if it stands for human rights, if it stands for the sanctity of international treaties, then I have come here to tell you that the Greek Cypriot armed elements in 1963 destroyed all these concepts in their attempt to destroy the Turkish Cypriot community. Since then, the Turkish Cypriot community has ruled itself, defying this jurisdiction in its own areas, in those areas where it was not eliminated. It has lived cut off from all the privileges of a State, cut off from all the rights of any human being. It has defied this jurisdiction because it thought that it was its duty to do so. But Mr Rolandis by sleight-of-hand has brushed all this aside and he has said that for the last 20 years the Turkish community is responsible for all that has happened to it. He has called for measures under the Charter in order to punish Turkey for having saved what he calls this guilty community. He has called for measures under the Charter to punish Turkey for having stopped the massacre of the Turks of Cyprus. He has said that such an action is necessary for peace in the island. Yes, for a peace of the graveyard for the Turkish Cypriots this is absolutely necessary. It is absolutely necessary that Turkey which came in at the last hour and saved the Turkish community should be drawn back so that under the title of the Government of Cyprus the Greek Cypriots can finish the work they began in 1963.

But he did not only say this; he did not only call for measures against Turkey. He tried by a variety of means which by now all members of the Council know very well to stop the Turkish Cypriots from being heard in this Council. But in case we were heard, he prophesied that the Turkish side would put on a theatrical spectacle in an effort to justify crime. He prophesied that the plight of the Turkish Cypriots would be mentioned again, and he said that the Turkish Cypriots have been the victims of their leaders and of Turkey for the last 20 years. He warned the Council about newspaper clippings which might be produced by us in proof of events in Cyprus.

In other words, Mr Rolandis tried to change the past. He tried to change the past completely. But a very wise Greek by the name of Aristotle stated that even God cannot change the past.

This past can be discovered not only from newspaper clippings, not only from the reports of the Secretary-General, but it can be discovered by a visit to Cyprus. This past is recorded in the household of every Turkish Cypriot in the form of a son or a father or a child, or a 90-year-old grandfather who has been lost to them because Greek Cypriots tried, with grave determination, to Hellenise Cyprus. This past is recorded in mass graves like Alloa, Marata and Sandalari, where 16-day-old babies rest arm-in-arm with their mothers, grandmothers and grandfathers; where elementary schools are shut because the whole elementary school population also was lined up and shot and crudely buried. Is it necessary for the Turkish Cypriots to bring newspaper clippings when we know what the facts are? Is it sufficient for Mr Rolandis to claim that the Turkish Cypriots are responsible for what has befallen them during the last 20 years?

The Turkish Cypriots themselves have to be convinced that the people talking on the other side of the bench are people who have changed in heart and who really seek peace, people who are not furthering their policy of Hellenising Cyprus by hook or by crook.

I have tried to alert the Special Political Committee to the fact that the title of the Government of Cyprus was being used as a tool of aggression against a quarter of the population of Cyprus, and that if a resolution, along the lines desired by the Greek Cypriots, emerged from the General Assembly, the beginning of the negotiations would thereby be hampered instead of facilitated. My prediction came true. The General Assembly passed a resolution which the Greek Cypriot side immediately used in order to avoid negotiations and to poison the climate in which the negotiations were to have been started. They immediately boasted that they had got so many votes, and that the General Assembly was with them, the reports of the Commission on Human Rights supported the Government of Cyprus, and the resolutions of the non-aligned countries were in favour of the Government of Cyprus. This was a futile attempt to change the past. These resolutions were one-sided resolutions. They cannot change the past. The reports of the Commission on Human Rights is a one-sided report which cannot cover up the facts of life in Cyprus. With regard to the resolutions of the non-aligned countries, the representatives of the non-aligned countries came to us soon after their adoption to explain how that had come about. In a bi-national country, where one of the nations – the Greek Cypriot nation – has tried to destroy the Turkish Cypriot nation, all these assemblies, commissions and conferences are closed to the victimised Turkish Cypriots. In an undefended football match the Greek Cypriots score goals by shooting the ball into an open goal undefended by any goalkeeper. Then they count the scores and tell the world that they are the winners. They have to convince us that they are our partners and that they are willing to play this game with us, not for scoring points in the international field, but for making peace in Cyprus. Scoring points in the international field by propaganda, by resorting to untruths, by misstating the facts cannot and will not bring about reconciliation between the two communities. Without reconciliation of the two communities there can be no peace in Cyprus.

I was heartened for a moment when I heard Mr Rolandis refer to Rudyard Kipling's poem, the famous 'If'. He referred to one part of it which spoke about waiting, and not being tired of waiting and he asked, 'for how long will Cyprus be subjected to injustice?' It is unfortunate that in Cyprus terms have two meanings. 'Justice' and 'injustice' unfortunately do not have the same meaning for the Turks and the Greeks. 'Justice' for the Greeks means Hellenisation of Cyprus, majority rule in Cyprus, allowing the Turkish Cypriots to go without guarantees, undefended, and to live at their mercy as hostages in what they call 'pre-aggression' days, pre-1974 days when Turkish Cypriots lived from day to day not knowing what would happen tomorrow. He says that Cyprus has been waiting for four years.

This statement in itself should tell something to the Security Council, which has been seized of the Cyprus problem not for four years, but for 15 years. The Turkish Cypriot community has been waiting for justice for 15 years, for the re-establishment of a bi-national Cyprus so that the security of the Turkish community should not be threatened again, so that Greek Cypriots would not have an opportunity of using us as hostages, or blackmailing Turkey by saying that if it dared to come to save the threatened Turks then it would find no Turks to save. Mr Rolandis read the words which speak of waiting:

If you can wait and not be tired by waiting, or being lied about, do not deal in lies,

I will read another part of this beautiful significant poem:

If you can dream and not make dreams your master, If you can think and not make thoughts your aim.

I read these lines in the name of a community that dreamed for 15 years – and keeps on dreaming, without making dreams its master – of a peaceful Cyprus in which Turkish Cypriots and Greek Cypriots would live in harmony. But to achieve it we must stop denying the past, we must stop re-writing the history of Cyprus in assemblies in which the Turkish Cypriot community is not present.

In the words of the Secretary-General, Mr Rolandis wants translation of the United Nations resolutions into reality. Who does not? Where will this world be if the United Nations resolutions are not translated into reality by all the people who are affected by them? But those who manoeuvre by using propaganda to bring about one-sided resolutions which if applied would mean the destruction of the innocent, the destruction of a bi-national country, even the destruction of an independence, have no right to claim that such resolutions have not been translated into reality, because the translation of such resolutions into reality would mean the destruction of every principle that the United Nations Charter was meant to protect and to cherish.

We saw Mr Rolandis in an acrobatic attempt trying to divide the issue into the internal aspect of the problem, namely the constitutional and territorial issue, and the external aspect, namely the question of aggression and foreign interference. It is 'interference' if under an international treaty one of the guarantor Powers risks everything in order to honour that treaty for the purpose of saving one of the nations which brought about the Republic of Cyprus.

Ponder for a moment what would have happened to Cyprus and to the Turkish Cypriots if Turkey had not moved. If representatives will merely ask themselves that question, I am sure they will see the true picture. If not, then we have the true picture on the soil of Cyprus, I repeat, in the form of mass graves, in the form of young people in their hundreds being called in to police stations to make statements and being destroyed, in the form of people who have been taken off the streets and have not reappeared in 15 years.

That is 'interference'. Stopping that kind of conduct for and on behalf of one of the nations which put their signatures to an agreement is interference in the internal affairs of Cyprus.

In his statement Mr Rolandis said,

We are a small country, and our ambitions are not and cannot be greater than our size (S/PV.2099, p. 11).

I thank God for that, because it appears that uniting Cyprus as a whole to Greece is an ambition compatible with the size of the Greek Cypriot community. Uniting Cyprus as a whole with Greece in spite of the objections of one fourth of the population, if necessary by eliminating all the Turkish Cypriot community, seems to be no ambition at all.

May I refer to a statement made by the late Archbishop Makarios on 21 August 1964, in which he said:

My ambition is to accomplish the union of Cyprus with Greece. I will unite Cyprus integrally with Greece and then the borders of Greece will extend to the shores of North Africa.

A small country with no ambition, of course, could not do better.

It appears that we should see no wrong ambition, no harmful ambition, in the attempt of the Greek Cypriot wing of a bi-national Government to project itself for 15 years as the Government of Cyprus. That is no ambition. The assertion that they can talk and defend the Turkish Cypriots also seems to be no ambition. A small defenceless country, we are told, was attacked by a major Power and destroyed, and it is seeking justice from you all. Smallness and strength are comparative terms.

When we faced 30,000 fully-armed Greek Cypriots helped by the Greek army from the mainland for years and years, the strength was massive, with tanks and all possible kinds of arms from all over the world. Turkey came in order to stop those people from destroying Cyprus and from destroying the Turkish Cypriot community. Turkey could not go there with walking sticks; it could not face those armaments

167

without arms. And now we are told that Turkey used force in maintaining the independence of Cyprus.

I will quote another passage by Archbishop Makarios. He said this on 29 July 1970. I quote Archbishop Makarios because the new leader of the Greek community has repeatedly stated that his policy and his way are the policy and way of Archbishop Makarios. The archbishop said:

> The hearts of the Greeks of Cyprus, of Rhodes, and of all the Dodecanese Islands have a common beat. You have achieved your aspirations, but we, beset by difficulties and frustrated by foreign meddlers, are still struggling for ours. But despite all difficulties Cyprus will march on to Hellenism.

A foreign meddler frustrated this march on to Hellenism. The foreign meddler is none other than Turkey, and the Turkish community, which defended its independence, its inalienable rights and the independence and sovereignty of Cyprus, is immediately labelled the agent of Turkey, and everything is done in order to stop it from being heard in the international arena.

But for this 'foreign meddling' Cyprus would have been part of Greece by now. To the Greeks, that is liberty, that is justice, that is freedom, that is a beautiful thing. No one asks what that is to the Turkish Cypriots of Cyprus, and that is the problem of Cyprus.

To divide the problem into internal and external factors, which Mr Rolandis tried to do in the Council, is a new attempt to avoid what they call foreign meddlers, meaning Turkey and the Turkish Cypriots, from arresting this march forward to Hellenism. There is a Chinese proverb which states: 'A long journey proves the stamina of a horse; the passage of time tells the heart of men.' After having listened to Mr Rolandis in the General Assembly and to Mr

Michaelides in the Special Political Committee, back to Mr Rolandis in the General Assembly and later in the Security Council, I can tell members of the Council that after 15 years there is no change of heart in the Greek Cypriot leadership, that the votes which they have contrived to obtain from the General Assembly have hardened them on this march forward to Hellenism. The architects of the Akritas Plan have not changed their vision of Cyprus. Even the threats are the same.

> Mr Rolandis asked the Council not to forget that volcanoes erupt. He said '. . . nothing in this world is more dangerous than to push people to the point of desperation.' (S/PV.2099 p. 11).

They are desperate. Why? Because 'foreign meddlers' have stopped this spurious march forward to Hellenism; because the agents of foreign meddlers, the Turkish Cypriot community, has dared to defend its rights in the independence and sovereignty of Cyprus and has refused to succumb to brute force. They do not even want us to talk about our plight from 1963 to 1974. We heard the same threat of volcanoes erupting in the 1955–8 period. Unless the road to Hellenism, to union with Greece, is opened, the volcano will erupt.

We then lived throughout Cyprus among Greek populations, and we suffered because of it. The same threat is the basis of the Akritas Plan. We had the same threat in 1965, again from Archbishop Makarios, who spoke at Rizokarpaso on 26 May 1965. He said:

> The whole of Cyprus is to be united with Greece or it will become a holocaust. The road to fulfilment of national aspirations may be full of difficulties, but we shall reach the goal, *Enosis*, alive or dead.

The fact that on this march to the goal Turkish Cypriots would suffer and would die was, of course, irrelevant. The Greek Cypriots do not like the fact that we objected to being killed in the name of that glorious march.

But now such threats do not affect us because, thanks to our redemption, thanks to the exchange of population which we carried out in the last phases with the help of the United Nations Peace-keeping Force in Cyprus (UNFICYP), we now live in our own sector, and if the Greek Cypriots erupt, they will have to suffer the consequences. We shall wait in our sector until that eruption ends. They will probably again fill lorries with their dead, killing each other as they did during the coup, taking them to the priests to have them buried at gunpoint, even when some of the presumed dead were still breathing.

But we hope that common sense and the long years of suffering and experience will teach them a few lessons. I hope the lesson that they will learn is that Cyprus is not destined to become a Greek Cypriot island. It is destined to become a Cypriot island on which Greeks and Turks shall live side by side and shall co-operate. The two communities shall live side by side and co-operate until a state of affairs is reached in which trust and confidence begin to grow.

Will this be understood by the Greek Cypriot side? I do not know. This long journey, this long struggle, I believe, has proved the stamina of the Turkish-Cypriot horse, if I may refer again to the Chinese proverb, and this passage of time tells us that the hearts of the Greek Cypriot leaders, unfortunately, have not changed.

It was with great regret that I listened to the statement by Mr Rolandis. I have come here in order to help to create an atmosphere and to work for a resolution which would help in the settlement of the Cyprus problem by enhancing the chances of the beginning of a resumption of the intercommunal negotiations. But Mr Rolandis thinks otherwise. He believes that the resolutions of the United Nations have given him the mandate to speak for the whole of Cyprus, including the Turkish community, which he has already equated with a small minority community of 2,500 in a Greek Cyprus. Government by consent means nothing to him. What they tried to do in 1963 and continued to do until 1974 is evidence of 'good government'. What happened to the Turkish Cypriots during that time was the fault of the Turkish Cypriot community. He does not understand that the 1963 armed onslaught against the Turkish Cypriots was an attempted coup against the bi-nationality of Cyprus and that that coup did not succeed fully because the Turkish Cypriot community continued to defend its rights, and it continues to defend its rights. He thinks that the coup was successful, that the bi-nationality of the Government is at an end, that the Greeks of Cyprus represent the Republic of Cyprus fully and that, therefore, the Cyprus problem is almost ended and will be completely disposed of as soon as United Nations resolutions demanding the withdrawal of Turkish troops from Cyprus are implemented.

Then the ground would be free for the Greek Cypriots to finish the work which they have set themselves to do under the Akritas Plan, namely, to free what they see as Greek Cyprus from Turkish Cypriots. This is the problem of Cyprus; this is where we are all interlocked.

The Turkish Cypriot community, reacting to all that was done to it during the years when ejected from the bi-national Government, brought about its own administration. It was called the Transitional Cyprus Turkish Administration. We had to govern ourselves; we could not live in a vacuum. In time this developed, and after the Turkish intervention – which was a godsend and saved Cyprus from utter calamity – the Turkish Cypriots claimed their right in the independence of Cyprus and tried to show this to the world and to the

Greek Cypriots by forming a State, which they named the Federated State of Cyprus. We hoped that within a few months the Greek Cypriots would join hands with us and bring about the Federal Greco-Turkish Republic of Cyprus. Four years have elapsed and the Greek Cypriots have preferred to go around collecting votes and resolutions from international forums in which the Turkish Cypriots are not represented.

What, then, is our remedy? I am appealing to the members of the Council as one of a people which has an inalienable right in the independence and sovereignty of Cyprus and whose right is being prejudiced through and by the resolutions of the world Assembly, because equal hearing is not given to the Turkish community. Are we going to succumb? Are we going to put our neck into the noose? Are we going to say that we give up defending our basic rights in the bi-national Republic of Cyprus? Is this what is expected of us, because this is what Mr Rolandis and his leaders expect of us?

I can do no better on this vital question than refer the Council to a historic document:

> When in the Course of human Events, it becomes necessary for one People to dissolve the Political Bands which have connected them with another, and to assume among the Powers of the Earth, the separate and equal Station to which the Laws of Nature and of Nature's God entitle them, a decent Respect to the Opinions of Mankind requires that they should declare the Causes which impel them to the Separation.

In this case, the Turkish Cypriot people has not chosen separation. It has been ejected from the Government of Cyprus by brute force. It has been kept out of it for 15 years. It has been denied all the rights and privileges of a Government and of a State. Those who call themselves 'the Government of Cyprus' have tried to destroy this co-partner community – and all this is in the records of the Security Council. If the Security Council is not aware of the truth, then there is no justice in this world. But I know that members are aware of the truth; I know that they are aware of what is happening in Cyprus.

So what can we do? I quote:

We hold these Truths to be self-evident, that all Men are created equal, that they are endowed by their Creator with certain unalienable Rights, that among these . . . Rights Governments are instituted among Men, deriving their just Powers from the Consent of the Governed, that whenever any Form of Government becomes destructive of these Ends, it is the Right of the People to alter or to abolish it, and to institute new Government, laying its Foundation on such Principles, and organising its Powers in such Form, as to them shall seem most likely to effect their Safety and Happiness. Prudence, indeed, will dictate that Governments long established should not be changed for light and transient Causes; and accordingly all Experience hath shown that Mankind are more disposed to suffer, while Evils are sufferable, than to right themselves by abolishing the Forms to which they are accustomed. But when a long Train of Abuses and Usurpations, pursuing invariably the same Object, evinces a Design to reduce them under absolute Despotism, it is their Right, it is their Duty, to throw off such Government, and to provide new Guards for their future Security.

I have no Government, the Turkish community has no Government, to overthrow. Those who call themselves 'the Government' have kept the Turkish community out by force for 15 years, and they come here to get a mandate from the

Council for tying the hands of this community so that they can finish what they started in 1963 and continued relentlessly until 1974. Will the Council give them this mandate? If it does, then we shall not be defying the Council – God forbid – but we shall be using our rights as the American people used theirs and put them in the Declaration of Independence, by not recognising an evil force as the Government of Cyprus. We are left with no alternative.

Need I at this stage go into pages and pages of what was done to us? I shall not take up the Council's time. I shall merely refer to a letter which was written by Dr Fazil Kuchuk, the then Vice-President of Cyprus, to all Heads of State in December 1963, because that also has become part of the past and because there has been an attempt to change that also.

> To all Heads of States,
>
> The Greeks of Cyprus, taking advantage of, and abusing their majority strength in the Government and Security Forces of the Republic, have planned and put into execution an organised armed attack by the Greek Police and civilians on the Turks and Turkish property in towns and villages, including my own residence and office, since the night of 20 December 1963.
>
> These attacks continued in a most brutal and barbarous manner until the intervention of the three Guaranteeing Powers. During these attacks Turkish houses in Nicosia and elsewhere have been broken into and many innocent Turks, including women and children, have been murdered in cold blood in their houses or driven away as hostages.
>
> The Greek leaders, who are misrepresenting to the world the true facts have, in complete disregard of our Constitution and Laws, illegally armed with heavy weapons the Greek members of the Security Forces and also thousands

of Greek terrorists while Turks holding political posts have been prevented deliberately from exercising their powers and functions and Turkish members of the Security Forces have been disarmed and placed under detention.

At the same time, Turkish citizens have been labelled by Greek leaders as rebels to be shot dead on sight if seen outside their houses or sectors.

Despite the cease-fire agreement, Turkish life and property are still in great and imminent danger in Cyprus.

Even after the cease-fire, Turks have been killed and kidnapped and many Turkish houses have been looted or maliciously set on fire by the Greeks. Turks both in towns and villages are still besieged and all means of communication have been cut off to them. Also, the normal supply of ₊oodstuffs to Turkish citizens is no longer possible.

Reliable reports reaching us indicate that, even now, the Greeks are arming and preparing another onslaught for a general massacre on a larger scale than before.

The Greek leaders have made it abundantly clear that at the impending London Conference they will not back an inch from their policy of complete domination of the Turks and of placing them at their mercy. For this purpose Archbishop Makarios has already made it public that he is determined to abrogate the Treaty of Guarantee. His ulterior motive in so doing is clearly to prevent Turkey from coming to the rescue of the Turkish Community in Cyprus when the ultimate Greek design of complete domination or extermination of Cypriot Turks is finally put into execution.

It is inconceivable that such brutal atrocities could have been committed and that such a state of affairs can be allowed to continue at this advanced stage of civilisation.

I, therefore, appeal to you and through you to all peace-loving nations of the world who believe in the inviolability of human rights and liberties and who disapprove of racial discrimination, violence and genocide to give their support, both material and moral, to the Turkish Cypriot Community in their struggle for survival against very heavy odds.

That was in late 1963. The Turkish Cypriots resisted all the evil forces of the Greek Cypriot leadership until 1974. Today, our life, our liberty, our rights in the independence and sovereignty of Cyprus are still at stake. I hope the Security Council will show Mr Rolandis and, through him, the Greek leadership that the votes of the General Assembly and of this Council do not entitle anyone to destroy one fourth of the population of a country, whatever name that sort of activity may be given.

I shall not take the Council's time any longer, Mr President. I hope that we shall be given an opportunity to give our views on the draft resolution which the Council may adopt. If this is the time to give it, I shall do so. But I do not know whether it is submitted or not. I wish to state the views of the Turkish Cypriot community on that draft resolution. Is this the time? I do not know.

With these words I should like once again to thank you, Mr President, for your patience and to thank the Secretary-General, his Special Representative in Cyprus, Mr Galindo Pohl, and all his associates and assistants, the UNFICYP Commander in Cyprus and his men for doing an excellent job for Cyprus and for trying their best to bring about the resumption of the intercommunal talks. It is only through the intercommunal talks that we see a hope for final peace in Cyprus and we hope that the resolution of this Council will not, like the resolution of the General Assembly, hinder the resumption of these talks, but will facilitate their resumption.

Further statement by Mr Denktash later in the debate.

DENKTASH: Mr Rolandis again spoke about unilateral action and about how that is disliked here in connection with the resolution which has just been adopted. I should like to state for the record that each time the Greek Cypriot section of the bi-national Government of Cyprus refers to itself as 'the Government' and takes any action as 'the Government', especially in international forums, against the Turkish Cypriots, we regard it as a unilateral action, and we consider that we are quite entitled to take a counter action for our protection. I think I gave sufficient notice of what that is to be in my first statement.

As regards the resolution which has just been adopted, I should like to underline that it makes reference to resolutions to which the Turkish Cypriot community had never been a party and on which it had not been heard. Those resolutions, therefore, were adopted in its absence. They have no bearing on the realities of the Cyprus situation and they contravene bilateral agreements which had been arrived at in the presence of the Secretary-General. Therefore, the implementation of those resolutions would mean undoing certain things which have been done and which have affected the lives of thousands of people, in compliance with other United Nations decisions, through the Secretary-General and through other officers. In that regard they are unrealistic and cannot be implemented. For example, the Turkish community cannot, just because a resolution says so, uproot itself for the fourth time in Cyprus and go back and become hostages in Greek Cypriot areas. That is utterly impossible and unrealistic and the Greek Cypriots should not deceive themselves that this can be done just because they had managed to have a one-sided resolution in their favour adopted at a time when we were not heard.

The time-limit is continually underlined by the Greek Cypriot side, which forgets that when the Cyprus problem was brought to the Security Council in February and March

1964, the time-limit which was then foreseen was three months. It was then extended for another three months and everybody thought that would be the end. We prayed that it would be the end because we were really suffering. But we have now come to the fifteenth year, and the time-limit is extended from six months to six months.

We want to abide by the resolutions of the Security Council and the resolutions of the General Assembly. However, to accomplish that, others should not seek and obtain resolutions which may not be in full accord with the realities appertaining to the problem. I do not want to go into the details of this, but I wish to say that this resolution will not be conducive to the beginning of the intercommunal negotiations. Indeed, we have the atmosphere reflected by what Mr Rolandis has just said, namely that when the time is up and when we come back here he is hopeful of obtaining a stronger, more effective resolution. Those who aim at that goal will naturally spend their time, as they have spent it in the past, not in negotiating a settlement but in finding flimsy excuses for prolonging the issue.

In the meantime, the Turkish Cypriot community looks upon Turkey as the motherland and as a guarantor and begs and demands that its protection should not be withdrawn from us. That is our request and I pass it on and place it on record with all the feeling in my heart.

Appendix 11 : *The Akritas Plan*

WHAT IS THE AKRITAS PLAN?

It is the plan of a conspiracy to dissolve the Republic of Cyprus, in pre-determined stages and methods, and to bring about the union of Cyprus with Greece.

The plan was drawn up by the Greek Cypriot leadership in collusion with Greek Army officers in 1963. It provides, among other things, for the creation of an underground army which, as explained in the 'Plan' would suppress any resistance by the Turks, most forcefully, and in the shortest possible time, and make the Greek Cypriots master of the situation **'within a day or two, before outside intervention would be possible, probable, or justifiable.'** The plan was signed by 'the Chief Akritas'. It also explains the object of the 13-point proposal put forward by Archbishop Makarios for the revision of the Constitution.

This top secret document was first published by a local Greek newspaper – *Patris* – on 21 April 1966, with the professed intention of exposing the mishandling of the Greek Cypriot national cause by Archbishop Makarios. In a series of articles published subsequently by the same paper, it was disclosed that Archbishop Makarios had assumed the responsibility for the implementation of the plan, and that he had appointed Mr Polycarpos Yorgadjis, who was the Minister of the Interior at the time, to be the Chief Akritas, together with other top ranking Greek members of the Government as officers of the secret organisation.

Certain parts of the English translation of the Plan presented here have been set in heavy type in order to underline those salient points which clearly show the relationship between the Plan and the various stages of the Cyprus crisis. This relationship is also very important from the point of view of the United Nations because it shows how the Greek Cypriot leaders, while paying lip service to the UN Charter and to its principles, were deviously trying to use the World Organisation as a tool to attain their objectives.

AKRITAS PLAN

TOP SECRET   HEADQUARTERS

Recent public statements by Archbishop Makarios have shown the course which our national problem will take in the near future. As we have stressed in the past, national struggles cannot be concluded overnight; nor is it possible to fix definite chronological limits for the conclusion of the various stages of development in national causes. Our national problem must be viewed in the light of developments which take place and conditions that arise from time to time, and the measures to be taken, as well as their implementation and timing, must be in keeping with the internal and external political conditions. The whole process is difficult and must go through various stages because factors which will affect the final conclusion are numerous and different. It is sufficient for everyone to know, however, that every step taken constitutes the result of a study and that at the same time it forms the basis of future measures. Also, it is sufficient to know that every measure now contemplated is a first step and only constitutes a stage towards the final and unalterable national objective which is the full and unconditional application of the right of self-determination.

As the final objective remains unchanged, what must be dwelt upon is the method to be employed towards attaining that objective. This must, of necessity, be divided into internal and external (international) tactics because the methods of the presentation and the handling of our case within and outside the country are different.

A. METHOD TO BE USED OUTSIDE

In the closing stages of the (EOKA) struggle, the Cyprus problem had been presented to world public opinion and to diplomatic circles as a demand of the people of Cyprus to exercise the right of self-determination. But the question of the Turkish minority had been introduced in circumstances that are known, intercommunal clashes had taken place and it had been tried to make it accepted that it was impossible for the two communities to live together under a united administration. Finally the problem was solved, in the eyes of many international circles, by the London and Zurich agreements, which were shown as solving the problem following negotiations and agreements between the contending parties.

(a) Consequently our first aim has been to create the impression in the international field that the Cyprus problem has not been solved and that it has to be reviewed.

(b) The creation of the following impressions has been accepted as the primary objective:

   (i)   that the solution which has been found is not satisfactory and just;

   (ii) that the agreement which has been reached is not the result of the free will of the contending parties;

(iii) that the demand for the revision of the agreements is not because of any desire on the part of the Greeks to dishonour their signature, but an imperative necessity of survival for them;

(iv) that the co-existence of the two communities is possible, and

(v) that the Greek majority, and not the Turks, constitute the strong element on which foreigners must rely.

(c) Although it was most difficult to attain the above objectives, satisfactory results have been achieved. Many diplomatic missions have already come to believe strongly that the Agreements are neither just nor satisfactory, that they were signed as a result of pressures and intimidations without real negotiations, and that they were imposed after many threats. **It has been an important trump card in our hands that the solution brought by the Agreements was not submitted to the approval of the people; acting wisely in this respect our leadership avoided holding a referendum. Otherwise, the people would have definitely approved the Agreements in the atmosphere that prevailed in 1959.** Generally speaking, it has been shown that so far the administration of Cyprus has been carried out by the Greeks and that the Turks played only a negative part acting as a brake.

(d) Having completed the first stage of our activities and objectives we must materialise the second stage on an international level. Our objective in this second stage is to show:

(i) that the aim of the Greeks is not to oppress the

Turks but only to remove the unreasonable and unjust provisions of the administrative mechanism;

(ii) that it is necessary to remove these provisions right away because tomorrow may be too late;

(iii) (Omitted)

(iv) that this question of revision is a domestic issue for Cypriots and does not therefore give the right of intervention to anyone by force or otherwise, and

(v) that the proposed amendments are reasonable and just and safeguard the reasonable rights of the minority.

(e) Generally speaking, it is obvious that today the international opinion is against any form of oppression, and especially against oppression of minorities. The Turks have so far been able to convince world public opinion that the union of Cyprus with Greece will amount to their enslavement. **Under these circumstances we stand a good chance of success in influencing world public opinion if we base our struggle not on ENOSIS but on self-determination.** But in order to be able to exercise the right of self-determination fully and without hindrance we must first get rid of the Agreements (e.g. the Treaty of Guarantee, the Treaty of Alliance, etc.) and for these provisions of the Constitution which inhibit the free and unbridled expression of the will of the people and which carry dangers of external intervention. For this reason our first target has been the Treaty of Guarantee, which is the first Agreement to be cited as not being recognised by the Greek Cypriots.

When the Treaty of Guarantee is removed no legal

or moral force will remain to obstruct us in determining our future through a plebiscite.

It will be understood from the above explanations that it is necessary to follow a chain of efforts and developments in order to ensure the success of our Plan. If these efforts and developments failed to materialise our future actions would be legally unjustified and politically unattainable and we would be exposing Cyprus and its people to grave consequences. Actions to be taken are as follows:

(a) The amendment of the negative elements of the Agreements and the consequent de facto nullification of the Treaties of Guarantee and Alliance. This step is essential because the necessity of amending the negative aspects of any Agreement is generally acceptable internationally and is considered reasonable (passage omitted) whereas an external intervention to prevent the amendment of such negative provisions is held unjustified and inapplicable.

(b) Once this is achieved the Treaty of Guarantee (the right of intervention) will become legally and substantially inapplicable.

(c) Once these provisions of the Treaties of Guarantee and Alliance which restrict the exercise of the right of self-determination are removed, the people of Cyprus will be able, freely, to express and apply its will.

(d) It will be possible for the force of the State (the Police Force) and in addition, friendly military forces, to resist legitimately any intervention internally or from outside, because we will then be completely independent.

It will be seen that it is necessary for actions from (a) to (d) to be carried out in the order indicated.

It is consequently evident that if we ever hope to

have any chance of success in the international field, we cannot and should not reveal or proclaim any stage of the struggle before the previous stage is completed. For instance, it is accepted that the above four stages constitute the necessary course to be taken, then it is obvious that it would be senseless for us to speak of amendment (a) if stage (d) is revealed, because it would then be ridiculous for us to seek the amendment of the negative points with the excuse that these amendments are necessary for the functioning of the State and of the Agreements.

The above are the points regarding our targets and aims, and the procedure to be followed in the international field.

B.   THE INTERNAL ASPECT

Our activities in the internal field will be regulated according to their repercussions and to interpretations to be given to them in the world and according to the effect of our actions on our national cause.

1.   The only danger that can be described as insurmountable is the possibility of a forceful external intervention. This danger, which could be met partly or wholly by our forces, is important because of the political damage that it could do rather than the material losses that it could entail. If intervention took place before stage (c), then such intervention would be legally tenable at least, if not entirely justifiable. This would be very much against us both internationally and at the United Nations. The history of many similar incidents in recent times shows us that in no case of intervention, even if legally inexcusable, has the attacker been removed by either the United Nations or the other powers without significant

concessions to the detriment of the attacked party. Even in the case of the attack on Suez by Israel, which was condemned by almost all members of the United Nations and for which Russia threatened intervention, the Israelis were removed but, as a concession, they continued to keep the port of Eliat in the Red Sea. There are, however, more serious dangers in the case of Cyprus.

If we do our work well and justify the attempt we shall make under stage (a) above, we will see, on the one hand, that intervention will not be justified and, on the other hand, we will have every support since, by the Treaty of Guarantee, intervention cannot take place before negotiations take place between the Guarantor Powers, that is Britain, Greece and Turkey. It is at this stage, i.e., at the stage of contacts (before intervention) that we shall need international support. **We shall obtain this support if the amendments proposed by us seem reasonable and justified. Therefore, we have to be extremely careful in selecting the amendments that we shall propose.**

The first step, therefore, would be to get rid of intervention by proposing amendments in the first stage. Tactic to be followed: (Omitted)

2. It is evident that for intervention to be justified there must be a more serious reason and a more immediate danger than simple constitutional amendments. Such reasons can be:

   (a) The declaration of ENOSIS before actions (a) to (c).
   (b) Serious intercommunal unrest which may be shown as a massacre of Turks.

The first reason is removed as a result of the Plan

drawn up for the first stage and consequently what remains is the danger of intercommunal strife. We do not intend to engage, without provocation, in massacre or attack against the Turks. Therefore, (section omitted) the Turks can react strongly and incite incidents and strife, or falsely stage massacres, clashes or bomb explosions in order to create the impression that the Greeks attacked the Turks and that intervention is imperative for their protection. Tactic to be employed: Our actions for amending the Constitution will not be secret; **we would always appear to be ready for peaceful talks** and our actions would not take any provocative and violent form. Any incidents that may take place will be met, at the beginning, in a legal fashion by the legal security forces, according to a plan. Our actions will have a legal form.

3. (Omitted)
4. It is, however, naive to believe that it is possible for us to proceed **to substantial actions for amending the Constitution, as a first step towards our more general Plan as described above,** without expecting the Turks to create or stage incidents and clashes. For this reason the existence and the strengthening of our Organisation is imperative because:

(a) if, in case of spontaneous resistance by the Turks, our counter attack is not immediate, we run the risk of having a panic created among Greeks, in towns in particular. We will then be in danger of losing vast areas of vital importance to the Turks, while if we show our strength to the Turks, immediately, and forcefully, then they will probably be brought to their senses and restrict their activities to insignificant, isolated incidents.

(b) In case of a planned or unplanned attack by the

187

Turks, whether this be staged or not, it is necessary to suppress this forcefully in the shortest possible time, since, if we manage to become the masters of the situation within a day or two outside intervention would not be possible, probable or justifiable.

(c) The forceful and decisive suppressing of any Turkish effort will greatly facilitate our subsequent actions for further Constitutional amendments, and it should then be possible to apply these without the Turks being able to show any reaction. Because they will learn that it is impossible for them to show any reactions without serious consequences for their community.

(d) In case of the clashes becoming widespread, **we must be ready to proceed immediately through actions (a) to (d), including the immediate declaration of ENOSIS, because, then, there will be no need to wait or to engage in diplomatic activity.**

5. In all these stages we must not overlook the factor of enlightening, and of facing the propaganda of, those who do not know or cannot be expected to know our plans, as well as of the reactionary elements. It has been shown that our struggle must go through at least four stages and that we are obliged not to reveal our plans and intentions prematurely. It is therefore more than a national duty for everyone to observe full secrecy in the matter. Secrecy is vitally essential for our success and survival.

This, however, does not prevent the reactionaries and irresponsible demagogues from indulging in false patriotic manifestations and provocations. Our Plan would provide them with the possibility of putting forward accusations to the effect that the aims of our leadership are not national and that only the amendment of the

Constitution is envisaged. The need for carrying out Constitutional amendments in stages and in accordance with the prevailing conditions, makes our job even more difficult. All this must not, however, be allowed to drag us to irresponsible demagogy, street politics and a race of nationalism. Our deeds will be our undeniable justification. In any case owing to the fact that, for well-known reasons, the above Plan must have been carried out and borne fruit long before the next elections, we must distinguish ourselves with self-restraint and moderation in the short time that we have. Parallel with this, we should not only maintain but reinforce the present unity and discipline of our patriotic forces. We can succeed in this only by properly enlightening our members so that they in turn enlighten the public.

Before anything else we must expose the true identity of the reactionaries. These are petty and irresponsible demagogues and opportunists. Their recent history shows this. They are unsuccessful, negative and anti-progressive elements who attack our leadership like mad dogs but who are unable to put forward any substantive and practical solution of their own. In order to succeed in all our activities we need a strong and stable government, **up to the last minute.** They are known as clamorous slogan-creators who are good for nothing but speech-making. When it comes to taking definite actions or making sacrifices they are soon shown to be unwilling weaklings. **A typical example of this is that even at the present stage they have no better proposal to make than to suggest that we should have recourse to the United Nations.** It is therefore necessary that they should be isolated and kept at a distance.

We must enlighten our members about our plans and objectives ONLY VERBALLY. Meetings must be held at the sub-headquarters of the Organisation to enlighten leaders and members so that they are properly equipped to enlighten others. NO WRITTEN EXPLANATION OF ANY SORT IS ALLOWED. LOSS OR LEAKAGE OF ANY DOCUMENT PERTAINING TO THE ABOVE IS EQUIVALENT TO HIGH TREASON. There can be no action that would inflict a heavier blow to our struggle than any revealing of the contents of the present document or the publication of this by the opposition.

Outside the verbal enlightenment of our members, all our activities, and our publications in the press in particular, must be most restrained and must not divulge any of the above. Only responsible persons will be allowed to make public speeches and statements and will refer to this plan only generally under their personal responsibility and under the personal responsibility of the Chief of sub-headquarters concerned. Also any reference to the written Plan should be done only after the formal approval of the Chief of the sub-headquarters who will control the speech or statement. But in any case such speech or statement MUST NEVER BE ALLOWED TO APPEAR IN THE PRESS OR ANY OTHER PUBLICATION.

The tactic to be followed: Great effort must be made to enlighten our members and the public VERBALLY. Every effort must be made to show ourselves as moderates. Any reference to our plans in writing, or any reference in the press or in any document is strictly prohibited. Responsible officials and other responsible persons will continue to enlighten the public and to increase its morale and fighting spirit without ever divulging any of our plans through the press or otherwise.

NOTE: The present document should be destroyed by burning under the personal responsibility of the Chief of the sub-headquarters and in the presence of all members of the staff within 10 days of its being received. It is strictly prohibited to make copies of the whole or any part of this document. Staff members of sub-headquarters may have it in their possession only under the personal responsibility of Chief of sub-headquarters, but in no case is anyone allowed to take it out of the office of sub-headquarters.

The Chief
AKRITAS

Appendix 12: *Explanatory Note of the Turkish Cypriot Proposals for the Solution of the Cyprus Problem, Presented to UN Secretary-General Dr Kurt Waldheim in Vienna on 13 April 1978*

The Turkish Cypriot and Greek Cypriot Communities, co-founders of the Republic of Cyprus:

Bearing in mind the experiences and sufferings of the past and in order to ensure their non-recurrence;

Determined to establish an independent, bi-zonal Federal Republic composed of two Federated States and to preserve the territorial integrity of Cyprus;

Agreeing in good faith to the founding of a partnership based on equality between the two Communities;

Aiming to serve the welfare of their members, enabling them to live side by side in peace and security, to enjoy the benefits and blessings of a democratic system of Government based on the rule of law and social justice and to enhance their social and economic development;

Being conscious of the fact that a democratic constitutional order based on the equal partnership of the two Communities is the most effective way of guaranteeing the protection of the human rights and fundamental liberties as embodied in the Universal Declaration of Human Rights, the European Convention for the Protection of Human Rights and Fundamental Freedoms and its Protocols, the International Covenant on Economic, Social and Cultural Rights, the International Covenant on Civil and Political Rights and its Optional Protocol;

Convinced of the historic necessity of following a policy of friendship and co-operation with their motherlands and of promoting good relations with all countries in conformity with the principle of non-alignment and with a sincere desire of preserving peace and security in the region;

Solemnly, by their own free will and agreement, adopt this Constitution.

The Preamble proposed by the Turkish Cypriot side for the Constitution of the Federal Republic of Cyprus.

EXPLANATORY NOTE OF THE TURKISH CYPRIOT PROPOSALS FOR THE SOLUTION OF THE CYPRUS PROBLEM

This document has been prepared for the purpose of explaining the Turkish Cypriot proposals, in a condensed form, on the following essential aspects of the Cyprus problem:

I.   The Federal Constitution.
II.   The Territories of the Federated States and a Proposal for a Joint Water Project.
III. Maraş (Varosha).

I. THE FEDERAL CONSTITUTION

This part includes the following essential aspects of the constitutional proposals:

A.   The common starting points of the constitutional solution.

B. Difficulties of the constitutional solution.
C. General observations on the Turkish Cypriot constitutional proposals for the establishment of a Federal Republic of Cyprus.

A. The Common Starting Points of the Constitutional Solution

A federal system of government for Cyprus is a solution which has been advocated by the Turkish Cypriot side from the very beginning of the intercommunal talks and has also been accepted by the Greek Cypriot side at the second summit meeting between President Denktash and Archbishop Makarios on the 12th February 1977 in the presence of the United Nations Secretary-General, Dr Kurt Waldheim.

The first point of the agreed instructions (guidelines) referred to in the communiqué issued at the end of this meeting stated that the two sides were 'seeking an independent, non-aligned, bi-communal Federal Republic'.

The first point of the proposals of the Greek Cypriot side submitted at the 6th round of the Vienna talks (31st March–7th April 1977) on the 'Basic Principles which should govern the Constitutional Structure of the Federal Republic of Cyprus' also referred to a 'federal republic consisting of the Greek Cypriot Region and the Turkish Cypriot Region' and thus recognised the 'bi-zonal' character of the Federation.

This means that the founding of an 'independent, sovereign, bi-communal and bi-zonal federal state' in Cyprus is a common starting point accepted by both sides. Furthermore, the text of the agreed instructions (guidelines) referred to in the communiqué issued at the end of the second summit meeting on the 12th February 1977 embodies an agreement on the 'non-aligned' character of the Federal Republic.

Consequently, there should be no difficulty in incorporating these agreed attributes in a basic definition of the new Federal Republic.

It is in this context that the Turkish Cypriot proposals contain provisions embodying these basic attributes and a Preamble expressing the common will of the two Communities **'to live side by side in peace and security, to enjoy the benefits and blessings of a democratic system of government based on the rule of law and social justice and to enhance their social and economic development'** and their determination to ensure the non-recurrence of the sufferings of the past.

B. Difficulties of the Constitutional Solution

In addition to obvious and well-known difficulties inherent in the formation of any federal system, such as reaching a compromise between the equality of partners, on the one hand, and the necessity of establishing a workable central government machinery, on the other, or striking a balance between the rights of the individuals and the interests of their respective communities, the 'federal question' in Cyprus involves many other crucial and deep-rooted problems.

I. POLITICAL DIFFICULTIES

(a) This is not a simple exercise of devolution of powers from an existing central government to its component parts, as is the case, for instance, in the devolution bill for Scotland, administrative regionalism in France or 'political decentralisation' of central powers to the Wallons and the Flemish in Belgium. **On the contrary, this is an effort to bring together two different Communities who lived through two decades of intercommunal**

violence and bloodshed (from 1955 when EOKA launched its terrorist campaign for Enosis until 1974 when Turkey intervened under the 1960 Treaty of Guarantee) and who now have their own distinct administrations, with their own legislative, executive and judicial organs, having exclusive control and authority over two distinct areas of the island.

(b) **This is not a search for a solution to a domestic 'national' problem, but a compromise between two conflicting 'national' demands of two different national Communities.** Throughout recent history, Greek Cypriots had looked upon Cyprus as a Greek land destined to be united with Greece while the Turkish Cypriots looked upon the island as an old Turkish land and adamantly refused to be colonised by Greece. To the Greek Cypriots union of Cyprus with Greece (Enosis) was 'liberation and freedom', to the Turkish Cypriots such a union was 'colonisation', loss of all human rights and physical elimination from Cyprus. Thus, the Greek Cypriot action for achieving Enosis always brought immediate reaction from the Turkish Cypriot side. Greece which coveted Enosis, helped the Greek Cypriots by giving them arms and personnel while Turkish Cypriots sought help from Turkey in self-defence.

Through the centuries the two national Communities had jealously guarded their national identity while each cherished is own 'national aspiration'. The Greek Orthodox Church preached Enosis and anti-Turkish sentiments while Greek Cypriot schools gave this 'national policy' further 'cultural' backing. The Turkish Cypriots took counter measures in order not to be eliminated or absorbed by the Greek Cypriot side.

It was inevitable, therefore, that the two Communities would come into violent collision when the Greek Cypriots, under the leadership of the Greek Orthodox Church, launched their terroristic campaign for achieving Enosis in 1955.

Contrary to the present Greek Cypriot propaganda, this campaign, which lasted until the end of 1958, was not for independence but for Enosis.

Then, in 1960, the two Communities accepted a compromise and worked out a Constitution after continuous deliberations which lasted for eighteen months. In short, the two national Communities, which had fought, for opposing political aims, agreed by the texts signed in Zurich and London, to forgo these aims in lieu of a 'partnership Republic' based on the existence of the two national Communities and on their inalienable rights and partnership status. These two Communities together brought about the 'bi-national' State of Cyprus. They together, under agreed terms of co-operation and partnership, shared the legislative, executive, judicial and other functions. Matters which the two Communities had managed on communal basis over the centuries – like education, religion, family law, etc. – were left to the autonomy of the Communal administrations which had legislative, executive, and judicial authority over such matters. In effect a 'functional federative system' had been established by the two co-founder Communities of the Republic.

This functional federative character of the former Republic of Cyprus is often forgotten by those who are apt to see the present search for a federal solution as an attempt to dismantle a completely 'unitary' system of government, which was not created or even envisaged by the 1960 Constitution.

2. SOCIO-ECONOMIC DIFFICULTIES

(a) The memories of the past events are still vivid in the minds of the people from both Communities. An element of mistrust and even of hostile suspicion exists on both sides.

The Greek Cypriot leadership in the past did not accept the 1960 Agreements as satisfying their 'national aspirations'.

Soon after independence, the Greek Cypriot side, knowing that the Turkish Cypriot Community would not abandon its rights and status, proposed amendments to the Constitution (November 1963) and when the Turkish Cypriot Community refused to agree to the proposed amendments they launched their attack in order to implement a well-prepared scheme which came to be known as 'the Akritas Plan'.

Turkish Cypriot houses and properties in 103 villages were destroyed. Nearly 30,000 Turkish Cypriots became refugees. In all areas where the Turkish Cypriot resistance continued an inhuman blockade was mounted. All Turkish Cypriots were physically barred from taking part in the administration of the island. All constitutionality was overboard. Turks of Cyprus lived at the mercy of Greek Cypriot and Greek mainland armed elements.

Turkish Cypriots lived on, resisting Greek Cypriot aggression from 1963 to 1974, never accepting the illegal Greek Cypriot rule – which claimed to be 'the Government of Cyprus' – as the legitimate government of the island.

Legitimacy could only be re-established when the two Communities came together under agreed terms of partnership. Greek Cypriots had, by resorting to violence, ousted the Turkish Cypriot partner from the administration.

On the 26th June 1967 the Greek Cypriot House of Representatives unanimously passed a resolution declaring that **'. . . it would not suspend the struggle . . . until this struggle ends in success through the union of the whole and undivided Cyprus with the motherland, without any intermediary stage'** and by the end of 1967 the Greek Cypriot armed elements who had combined to form one single task force with 20,000 Greek army personnel clandestinely brought to Cyprus attempted to finish off the Turkish Cypriot resistance by attacking the Turkish Cypriot inhabitants of Geçitkale (Kophinou) and Boğaziçi (Ayios

Theodoros). This activated Turkey to come to the aid of the Turkish Cypriots. In order to avert Turkey's intervention the attack on Turkish Cypriots was stopped and Greek Cypriot leaders agreed to have intercommunal talks which began in June 1968. These talks lasted – on and off – until the coup of July 1974, but although near-agreements were reached, several times the Greek Cypriot leadership refused to settle the problem on the basis of an 'intercommunal partnership Republic' guaranteed against Enosis.

The events which preceded the coup of July 1974 again meant further distress for the beleaguered Turkish Community whose members were used as political hostages by both sides of the inter-Greek conflict. In the end, the coup materialised. No one doubted that the coup was a final attempt for the take-over of the island by Greece and the destruction of the independence of Cyprus. Thousands of Greeks were killed by the coupists, but as usual Turkish Cypriots were inflicted sufferings at the hands of the Greeks. More Turkish Cypriot villages had to be abandoned, thousands more Turkish Cypriots became refugees. Had Turkey failed to move under and by virtue of the Treaty of Guarantee then Cyprus as an independent State would no longer be. The coup in Nicosia would consolidate the position of the Junta in Athens and extend its hegemony to Cyprus.

Turkey was left with no alternative but to move under the Treaty of Guarantee.

Inevitably the Turkish intervention of 1974, with the unavoidable consequences of any such military action, brought also sufferings to the Greek Cypriot Community who had to abandon their homes and emigrate. This was mainly due to the second phase of the operation on the 14th–16th August 1974 which, contrary to what the Greek Cypriot side would have world public opinion wrongly to believe, became imperative upon the massacre of Turkish Cypriot

199

civilians and the Greek Cypriots' refusal to fulfil the conditions of the Geneva Declaration of the 30th July 1974 –

— to establish a security zone at the limit of the areas under the control of the Turkish Armed Forces;
— to immediately evacuate all the Turkish Cypriot enclaves occupied by the Greek or Greek Cypriot forces;
— to exchange or release the detained military personnel and civilians.

Subsequently contacts and negotiations took place between the two sides from 1974 to 1977. It was agreed that the parties should work for a bi-communal, bi-zonal solution.

At the third Vienna talks in the summer of 1975 the parties agreed to exchange their population on a voluntary basis. UNFICYP undertook to help in this exchange programme and in the end half of the Turkish Cypriot population which had lived under most inhuman conditions in Greek Cypriots areas for eleven years moved North, while the majority of the Greek Cypriots in the North moved into Turkish villages and properties in the South.

A constitutional solution for Cyprus has to be evolved in the spectre of such a dramatic recent history and the main preoccupation in the minds of the people directly involved is to find ways of preventing the recurrence of the sufferings of the past.

(b) The two Communities coming together to establish a new form of government with the hope of preventing the recurrence of the past sufferings have not yet reached the same level of economic and social development.

The Turkish Cypriot Community, having first lived under a Greek Cypriot dominated government and then in isolated enclaves and forced today to cope with international restrictions imposed on its external communications, is economically weak and in need of creating its own viable economy and promoting its human potentialities. Starting with the events of 1963, all the economic resources of the island were utilised for the development of the Greek Cypriot Community, while governmental policies of customs, taxation, credit and investment were devised and implemented without any consideration of the economic development needs of the Turkish Cypriot Community. By a 'Government' Decree, sale of land to the Turkish Cypriots was prohibited while licences for building factories, etc. were arbitrarily denied to them. The Turkish Cypriots were deprived of their freedom of movement and communication and lived in an economy of consumption in their enclaves at the mercy of the Greek Cypriot producers and importers.

The Greek Cypriot Community, on the other hand, although having undergone the adverse affects of a recent armed conflict lives in a stronger economy, having enjoyed for at least a decade all the benefits of an administration with wide international recognition and trade relations. In this context it is worth recording that the Greek Cypriot administration, having deprived the Turkish Cypriot popution of its rightful share from the budget, forced the Turkish Cypriot population, which was left destitute, to import hard currency as aid from Turkey to the tune of 13 million pounds sterling per year all of which enriched the Greek Cypriot Central Bank for eleven years.

Today, as a consequence of the past situations and the usurpation of the governmental machinery by force of arms, external trade is still mainly in the hands of the Greek Cypriot Community who continue to retain the monopoly of representing foreign firms and enterprises on the island; the Greek Cypriot Community benefits from the privilege of signing bilateral trade agreements, financial and technological co-operation and extensive foreign aid at the international

level; it maintains regular commercial relations with the
EEC, the Commonwealth, the Socialist bloc and the non-
aligned countries and is in a position to attract the capital
and the know-how of foreign investors. Most of the
foreign aid, in terms of grants, credits and goods provided for the island, goes to the Greek Cypriot Community.

In addition, the economic blockade imposed by the Greek
Cypriots, as a deliberate instrument of policy, with the un-
witting backing of the international community, has further
aggravated the economic plight of the Turkish Cypriot
Community.

These discrepancies and inequalities in economic and social
conditions, coupled with the mistrust resulting from the vivid
memories of the past, are perhaps the most important difficulties on the way to establishing a federation in Cyprus.

3. LEGAL DIFFICULTIES

**(a) The federal principle implies, almost by de-
finition, an equality of partner states.** This is the main
guarantee under which different political entities agree to
enter into a political partnership. Yet, this principle of
equality carries the risk of creating deadlocks in the effective
operation of the governmental machinery established to
meet the administrative needs of the people at federal or
federated levels.

In decision-making, this difficulty is normally overcome
by subjecting the will of a smaller number of states to the
will of the greater number of states, regardless of their size
and population (e.g. simple majority of states, two-thirds of
states, nine out of thirteen, etc.)

**The difficulty in Cyprus is that the number of
states to be federated is only two and the principle
of equality of partners is therefore an absolute**

necessity imposed both by the principles of federalism and the duality of partners.

(b) **In this given situation the only way to reduce the risk of deadlock in the effective operation of the governmental machinery established to meet the administrative needs of the people is to reduce the number of functions to be carried out by the federal organs where this risk exists.** Therefore, there is an evident logical contradiction in the acceptance of the federal principle, on the one hand, and the insistence on creating a strong federal central administration, on the other hand, in a 'bi-communal' situation. Since it is clearly desirable for each equal partner to be able to run as much of its own affairs as possible without the blocking of the other, there is an obvious advantage in retaining essentially common functions as federal and leaving the residual powers to the federated states.

C. General Observations on the Turkish Cypriot Constitutional Proposals for the Establishment of a Federal Republic of Cyprus.

The Turkish Cypriot constitutional proposals for the establishment in Cyprus of an independent, sovereign, bi-communal, bi-zonal and non-aligned Federal Republic take into account the background to the Cyprus problem and the events which have taken place in Cyprus, particularly the period of violence and bloodshed during the past quarter of a century, and are designed to find a remedy for the past difficulties and to remove the obstacles in the way of a peaceful co-existence of the two national Communities, side by side, in a spirit of mutual trust and co-operation.

I. BASIC GUIDELINES

(a) The constitutional proposals take into account the

four guidelines which were agreed at the summit meeting of the 12th February 1977, between President Denktash and the late Archbishop Makarios, when the two leaders declared that they were 'seeking an independent, non-aligned, bi-communal, Federal Republic'. The following is the full text of the above-mentioned four guidelines:

'1. We are seeking an independent, non-aligned, bi-communal, Federal Republic.
2. The territory under the administration of each community should be discussed in the light of economic viability or productivity and land ownership.
3. Questions of principles like freedom of movement, freedom of settlement, the right of property and other specific matters, are open for discussion taking into consideration the fundamental basis of a bi-communal federal system and certain practical difficulties which may arise for the Turkish Cypriot Community.
4. The powers and functions of the central Federal Government will be such as to safeguard the unity of the country, having regard to the bi-communal character of the State.'

(b)   As explained above, there has existed in Cyprus since 1963, and, in the absence of a settlement, there still continues to exist, two separate and distinct Administrations representing the two national Communities, the co-founders of the Republic, respectively. This fact has been recognised by the three States guaranteeing the independence of the Republic of Cyprus, namely Turkey, Greece and Britain, by their Declaration at Geneva on the 30th July 1974, which stated that –

'The Ministers noted the existence in practice in the Republic of Cyprus of two autonomous administrations, that of the Greek Cypriot Community and that of the Turkish Cypriot Community. Without any prejudice to the conclusions to be drawn from this situation the Ministers agreed to consider at their next meeting the problems raised by their existence.'

In fact the intercommunal character of the conflict since 1955 and the bi-communality of the Republic which has reigned since 1960 is the underlying reality and foundation of all UN Resolutions since 1963.

The two separate, distinct and equal Administrations which exist in Cyprus today, exercise, in their respective areas, the full powers of the Republic. It follows therefore that in the establishment of the Federation, the Turkish Cypriot side is not starting off with an existing legitimate central government exercising full powers and functions over the whole Republic. The question is not which of these powers and functions should be devolved to the member states of the Federation, but, on the contrary, which of the powers and functions now being exercised by the already existing separate and distinct Administrations should be transferred to the central government.

(c) It is also an indisputable fact that when the powers and functions of a strong central government have been in the hands of a Greek Cypriot dominated government, the Turkish Cypriots have been treated as second class citizens and their human rights have been gravely and unjustly violated. **It is, therefore, imperative that in order to give the proposed new Federation a chance to survive, the constitutional arrangements must be such as to ensure that the tragic events of 1968–1974 should not, and cannot, be repeated again.** This logical, realistic and basic precautionary element has also been borne in mind in the preparation of the Turkish Cypriot constitutional proposals.

The Turkish Cypriot side sincerely wishes to unite the existing separate Administrations in a Federation, whereby the two Communities can co-exist, side by side, and co-operate with each other in a spirit of mutual trust and confidence.

The Turkish Cypriot proposals endeavour to achieve a political compromise between the conflicting interests and demands of the political units which compromise the Federation.

Above all, they aim to strike a balance, as in all democratic forms of government, between the rights and liberties of individuals, on the one hand, and the necessities of the governmental structure created for their administrative needs, on the other hand. The essence of the approach being the protection of the individual, the relationship between the founding communities is so regulated as to prevent the individual from becoming the victim of any settlement based on the supremacy of one community. The equality of the Communists, which is the salient feature of the Turkish Cypriot proposals, is based on no other consideration than that of protecting the individual from the consequences of an uneven intercommunal situation.

2. FUNDAMENTAL PREREQUISITES

Any workable solution for the constitutional order in Cyprus should, therefore, meet the following conditions:

(a) Deterrent guarantees against the recurrence of the past bloodshed, in order to secure, for each individual, the freedom from fear;

(b) Effective guarantees and machinery for the protection of human rights and liberties of all the individuals;

(c) The protection of each individual from political, economic and social discrimination and oppression resulting from membership of one community;

(d) The right of the members of each community to benefit equally from the opportunities, potentialities and protection of a state;

(e) The right of the members of each community to economic and social development and to prosperity on the territory of their own community;

(f) The protection of each community, as such, against the domination of the other community;

(g) The right of each community to preserve and develop its cultural, economic and commercial connections with the whole family of nations and particularly with its own motherland.

The ultimate aim of any democratic system of government being to ensure the safety of its citizens and to protect their inalienable rights of life, liberty and the pursuit of happiness, any attempt for a constitutional solution for Cyprus can only be meaningful if it takes into account all the above considerations together and establishes a harmony between them. It is, therefore, wrong to say, for instance, that the freedom of movement, freedom of residence, the right to property and free exercise of profession are essential for the acceptance of any solution by one side if the immediate and unconditional exercise of the same freedoms and rights are detrimental to the other fundamental prerequisites which are as essential and vital, if not more so, for the other side.

That is why the four guidelines which were agreed at the summit meeting of the 12th February 1977 between President Denktash and the late Archbishop Makarios, while referring to 'questions of principles like freedom of movement, freedom of settlement, the right of property and other specific matters' also stated that any discussion of these should take into consideration 'the fundamental basis of a bi-communal federal system and certain practical difficulties which may arise for the Turkish Cypriot Community'. The four guidelines also envisage the taking into account of 'economic viability or productivity and land ownership' when discussing territory.

The merit of any federal solution lies exactly in the variety of the ways in which different 'fundamentals' can be combined and compromised. It is equally wrong to insist upon the recognition of certain abstract principles and rules of government when such principles and rules lead to situations which create more deadlock and conflict rather than bring about practical and acceptable solutions for the welfare of the individual, from whichever community he may be.

3. BASIS OF THE FEDERAL STRUCTURE

The equality of the founding communities, however important, is not by itself a sufficient guarantee for the protection of the individual. That is why the Turkish Cypriot proposals put great emphasis on the judicial protection of the fundamental rights and liberties. Not only are these enumerated in an even more detailed way than in the 1960 Constitution, but a federal system of judicial review is established as a guarantee against their infringement by federal legislation. Moreover, the Federated States shall bear the domestic and international responsibility resulting from the violations of fundamental rights and liberties within their respective jurisdictions.

In a federative system, the protection of the individual in any community should also be envisaged in terms of his entitlement to benefit equally from the opportunities, potentialities and protection of a state which should be capable of providing him with essential services without interference from other communities who are partners in the union. This is especially important in a federation of only two communities who, by virtue of the federal principle, have come together on a basis of equality. **In a situation of mutual mistrust where each community has reservations about the goodwill of the other side, to start with the creation of a federal system with strong central powers covering a wide range of common functions is in fact asking for frequent tensions and interminable deadlocks.** These would result in the deprivation of the individuals from the benefits of governmental activities even in the stronger and more self-confident community, because such activities may continuously be subject to disruption or interference from the other partner.

Thus, the constitutional proposals of the Turkish Cypriot side have been made having regard to the existing realities and in the light of past experience. It is, therefore, proposed that the two existing separate Administrations should give up to the Federal Government only those basic powers and functions which are considered necessary and feasible for the purpose of maintaining common services and without security risks to the life and property of the inhabitants of the member states. If, in the course of time, it is proved by the conduct of all concerned that mutual trust and confidence can be built upon the initial links existing between the Federal Government and the two member States, then it is to be hoped that, with the growth of such confidence and with the elimination of mistrust and suspicion, it will be possible to strengthen such links by building upon them by the gradual transfer of additional powers and functions to the Federal Government. It is the sincere belief of the Turkish Cypriot side that the proposed Federation can only work and hope to survive, in the present circumstances, by starting cautiously and then build upon and strengthen the existing links and structures with the growth of mutual confidence.

In fact, in the case of some federations, the partners have set off on the federative venture even more cautiously and instead of starting off with a federal structure at the beginning they have started with a confederation. Two typical examples of this natural trend may be found in the case of the United States of America and the Swiss Federation which evolved from a confederal structure into a federation.

These two examples clearly show that when there is no confidence between the parties concerned – and this confidence is not something which can be imposed but must develop naturally and progressively between the partners – less power is given to the central authority. However, **as confidence between the parties grows, the powers of the central or federal government are increased by stages. This principle of 'growth of federation by evolution' is one of the basic principles of the Turkish Cypriot constitutional proposals.**

Another example which proves the same point from a different angle is the case of Yugoslavia: the strong control that the Federal Government had over the Federated Republics, a characteristic feature of the 1946 Constitution, proved inadequate and subsequent Constitutions and amendments gave much greater rights and powers to the Federated Republics which provided a much sounder basis for the edification of the successful federative experience in Yugoslavia.

In the light of its own experience and the experiences of others, the Turkish Cypriot side, in its desire to commence the new partnership venture with a federation which will eventually evolve into a stronger partnership, cannot ignore the tragic events of the past and risk the breaking down of the federation by not proceeding cautiously or by imposing too much of a strain on the central government.

4. THE FEDERAL STRUCTURE

For the fulfilment of federal functions enumerated in detail in the constitutional proposals as to their content and progressive implementation, the Turkish Cypriot side proposes the following structure:

(a) The Federal Executive. For reasons of equality, lack of confidence between the two Communities and the bitter experiences of the past which have been explained above, the joint direction of the Federal Executive by the two Presidents of the Federated States has been considered to be the fundamental basis of the smooth functioning of the executive organ. Undoubtedly the understanding, co-operation, collaboration and progressive creation of mutual trust and confidence between the two Communities has been shown to be best secured when the consensus of their leaders has been possible. The continuous joint participation of the two leaders on the basis of equality in the basic decision-making process for federal functions will greatly enhance the chances of obtaining the desired consensus.

Any other conception or approach that would place the two leaders on an unequal footing or force them to perform completely separate functions for federal matters would undermine the type of federation proposed and tend to create further polarisation between the two Communities.

It should be noted that equal representation of two numerically unequal communities in a joint federal executive is not a completely novel solution. Czechoslovakia gave the example, where the Prime Ministers of the Czech and Slovak Federated States took part in the federal executive as Vice-Premiers on an equal basis, although their communities represented approximately 65% and 29% respectively of the total population.

However, even in the case of such dual executive, there will be certain **ceremonial** and **formal** functions for which a single representation of the Federal State by the President of the Federal Republic is necessitated by the circumstances, in which case the Turkish Cypriot proposals foresee a two-yearly rotation between the two Presidents of the Federated States. A distinction should be made, however, between the proposal made here and the concept of alternation of a strong presidential office. The alternation of purely ceremonial and formal functions would not entail any substantial inconvenience in the functioning of the federal machinery.

(b) Federal Legislation. The type of federation proposed by the Turkish Cypriot side envisages separate Legislative Assemblies in the respective Federated States which shall deal with most of the legislative matters concerning life on the island. These Assemblies, being the elected representative organs of the two Communities, will also be enrolled in federal legislation covering common specific functions essential for a federal system of government, which are:

— Foreign Affairs;
— External Defence;
— Banking, Foreign Exchange and Monetary Affairs;
— Federal Budget;
— Customs Duties and Tariffs;
— External Communications;
— Federal Health Services;
— Standards of Weights and Measures, Patents, Trade Marks, Copyright and Meteorological Services;
— Tourism and Information.

In case of conflict in matters of federal legislation between the two Legislative Assemblies, provision has been made for the creation of a Federal Assembly composed of twenty members, ten from each Legislative Assembly. The system is so devised as to prevent the domination of one Community by the other and to eliminate the possibility of a complete deadlock. In addition to recourse to the Federal Constitutional Court on grounds of constitutionality, provision is also made, as a last resort, for submission to a referendum to be held separately in each Federated State.

(c) The Federal Constitutional Court. As pointed out above, in view of the importance attached to the protection of the rights and liberties of the individual in each Community, the Federal Constitutional Court is a basic feature of the Turkish Cypriot proposals. It shall be composed of six judges in equal numbers from each Federated State. The Federal Constitutional Court, in addition to its jurisdiction in constitutional matters, shall also act as the highest administrative court in federal matters.

5. OTHER BASIC FEATURES OF THE CONSTITUTIONAL PROPOSALS

The Turkish Cypriot side feels it imperative to include in the Federal Constitution provisions on the following matters –

(a) Reference to the 1960 Treaty of Guarantee and the Treaty of Alliance, as amended, thus giving them constitutional force;
(b) Entrenchment of the basic articles guaranteeing the independence, sovereignty, non-alignment of the bi-communal and bi-zonal Federal Republic and the unity of the country;
(c) Reservations on amendments for a period of seven years in order to give a fair chance to the new constitutional order;
(d) Establishment of a machinery for progressive implementation of federal functions on economic and social matters in accordance with the concept of 'growth of federation by evolution';
(e) Claims arising out of rights of ownership acquired prior to the Constitution shall be settled, together with all

other claims between the two Communities in the form
of debts, dues and compensation, by agreement between
the parties concerned;

(f) Rotation of certain basic federal functions between the
members of the two Communities in accordance with
the principle of equality and in order to reduce the
risks of deadlock.

II. THE TERRITORIES OF THE FEDERATED STATES AND A PROPOSAL FOR A JOINT WATER PROJECT

It has to be recognised that the question of territory is
closely related to the economic viability of both Communities
and to the question of security. This problem was taken up
between President Denktash and Archbishop Makarios at
their meeting on 12th February 1977 and it was decided that
the question of territory should be discussed 'in the light of
economic viability or productivity and land ownership'.
'Security' was the underlying principle on which these four
guidelines were based.

Therefore, it would be unrealistic to regard this problem
from the viewpoint of percentages of population alone. Half
of the whole Turkish Cypriot population has moved from
South to North. Greek Cypriots have moved from North to
South and an agreement for a voluntary exchange of
population was reached in the Third Round of the intercommunal talks, whereby the two parties recognised that
such an exchange was inevitable for the peaceful co-existence
of the two Communities in Cyprus. The approach to the
territorial problem, therefore, should be humanitarian and
pragmatic having regard to this accepted necessity so that
people who have been re-settled after so many years of
suffering should not be uprooted again. Where this is not

fully possible one should settle the problem in such a way that a minimum number of people should be uprooted once again. Otherwise the movement of Turkish Cypriots from South to North would have been meaningless and their security needs would be totally ignored.

The Turkish Cypriot side is prepared to discuss the question of territory taking into consideration the above mentioned facts and within the context of the aforesaid guidelines agreed upon by President Denktash and Archbishop Makarios.

Furthermore, while considering the territorial aspect of the problem it would be appropriate to bear in mind the following:

(a) The Turkish Cypriot Community is predominantly an agricultural society. Hence, the proportion of Turkish Cypriots depending on land is far greater than that of Greek Cypriots.

(b) Almost all direct or indirect foreign economic assistance given to Cyprus by international organisations since 1963 and more particularly since 1974 has almost exclusively been channelled to the Greek Cypriot Community.

(c) As a result of the systematic policy of economic oppression pursued by the Greek Cypriot Administration against the Turkish Cypriot Community since 1963, the economic development level of the Turkish Cypriot Community has remained far below that of the Greek Cypriot Community. While re-adjusting the existing line caution should be exercised so that the transfer of economic resources from the economically poorer to the richer Community would not further widen the economic gap and increase the tension between the two Communities.

When considering the proposals for the re-adjustment of

the existing line between the Turkish Cypriot and Greek Cypriot zones, the following relevant economic facts should also be taken into account:

1. Of forests only 22.6% fall within the Turkish Cypriot territory and the remaining 77.4% fall within the Greek Cypriot territory. The forests in the Greek Cypriot territory have been about 95% more productive than the forests of the Turkish Cypriot territory.

2. Of about 40 existing streams only a quarter are situated in the Turkish Cypriot territory. There are only 8 active dams and reservoirs in the Turkish Cypriot area with a total storage capacity of 8 million cubic metres of water compared with 45 on the Greek Cypriot side with a total storage capacity of nearly six times as great.

3. The annual average rainfall is approximately three times higher on the Greek Cypriot side than on the Turkish Cypriot side.

4. As for the aquifers, two of the three main ones in the Turkish Cypriot area are already depleted and faced with destruction. Sea water has penetrated and salinised most of the Gazi Mağusa (Famagusta) aquifer and the important part of the land in the area was dried up some years ago. The Güzelyurt (Morphou) aquifer faces the prospects of total loss in the immediate future unless serious precautions at the expense of millions of pounds are taken. On the contrary the aquifers on the Greek Cypriot side offer excellent prospects for utilisation and development.

5. Approximately 90% of the principal mines and quarries of economic value are situated in the Greek Cypriot area.

6. The only petroleum refinery is situated in the Greek Cypriot area.

7. The Mesarya (Messaoria) plain is dry land giving one yield of crop on alternate basis a year so that half of the area is not cultivated each year whereas in the south

land is irrigated and yields crop at least twice a year.
8. With more water made available land in both sectors
    can be made more productive so that the prosperity of
    the island as a whole is increased. A project costing
    about 150–200 million dollars for bringing water from
    Turkey to Cyprus is proposed by the Turkish Cypriot
    side as a matter for serious consideration.

With the above considerations in mind the Turkish Cypriot
side is ready to enter into negotiations with the Greek
Cypriot side for re-adjusting the line existing between the
Turkish Cypriot and Greek Cypriot zones in Cyprus.

III. MARAŞ (VAROSHA)

Due to the fact that Greek Cypriot armed elements chose to
use Maraş (Varosha) and the high buildings within it as
attack posts against the Turkish Cypriot population of Gazi
Mağusa (Famagusta) where 14,000 Turkish Cypriots, including women and children, were trapped and suffered
extensive casualties within the walled city from 20th July to
14th August, 1974, it became necessary for security reasons
to extend the forward lines south of Maraş (Varosha).

Ever since Maraş (Varosha) has remained uninhabited,
Turkish Cypriot endeavours to bring back some or all of the
hoteliers and other businessmen in order to activate the town
and save the properties from destruction by the elements
were fruitless because Greek Cypriot leaders, for political
reasons, prevented these people from returning to their
properties.

The Turkish Cypriot side approaches the problem in ways
which will enable a great number of Greek Cypriot owners
to return to their properties, subject to certain conditions,
while taking care of the security requirements of the Turkish

217

Cypriots – particularly those living in Gazi Mağusa (Fama-gusta), both within and outside the City Walls, as well as the security requirements of the Harbour, being the main commercial port of the Turkish Cypriot Community – and at the same time settling the problem, within the four guidelines agreed upon by the two leaders on 12th February 1977.

Postscript

Due to unforeseen difficulties the publication of this book has been delayed by almost two years. It is, therefore, necessary to add a few words about recent developments in Cyprus in order to bring the reader up to date.

The intervening period, not unfortunately but not unexpectedly, witnessed perceptible progress towards a solution of the inter-communal conflict. The Greek Cypriot leaders continue to hope that by shouting 'invasion' they will be able to consolidate their attempts to destroy the bi-communal partnership status of the Republic while the Turkish Cypriots continue to demand the re-establishment of the partnership Republic in a bi-zonal federal system. In the meantime, the advent of Mr Andreas Papandreou to the premiership, his perception of Cyprus as 'an extension of Greece which has to be redeemed from the Turks' and his preference for 'the internationalisation' of the problem at the expense of the intercommunal talks have put new difficulties in the way of these talks. So the question posed for Cyprus (and the world) continues to be whether the island shall revert to its new agreed bi-zonal federal form or whether the two national communities shall continue to be a cause of conflict not only between themselves but also between their respective motherlands, Turkey and Greece.

Lefkosa
March, 1982

Index